OF THE
RIVER
PEOPLE

Memories of a Midland childhood

OF THE
RIVER
PEOPLE

Memories of a Midland childhood

Anthony Perry

BREWIN BOOKS

BREWIN BOOKS
56 Alcester Road,
Studley,
Warwickshire,
B80 7LG
www.brewinbooks.com

Published by Brewin Books 2015

A CIP catalogue record for this book is available from the
British Library.

ISBN: 978-1-85858-534-5

Printed and bound in Great Britain
by 4edge Ltd.

Contents

Bibliography, Acknowledgements and Further Reading

Cinemas of the Black Country
Ned Williams, 1982

Empire Palace of Varieties
David Clayton, 1990

House of Fraser – Beatties Department Store Heritage Room
Mark Jones

History of Wolverhampton to the Early Nineteenth Century
Gerald Mander and Norman Tildesley, 1960

The Author Wishes to Thank the Following People

My mother and father, Phyllis and Kenneth Perry, and members of the families no longer with us

My wife Joyce for her help, patience and caretaking

Gladys Averill and Karen White

Wolverhampton Archives and Local Studies

Glenis Coates

Lee Amphlett

Amphlett One Name Study Group – Marion Carolan

Jean Wilson

Collegiate Church of St Peter, Wolverhampton

Millie Edwards

Worcestershire County Archives – Mike Quarrell

Pamela Brogan and Sara Scargill for their research work

Barry Noakes

Brewin Books – Alan Brewin

National Archives

House of Fraser – Beatties Department Store – Debbie Eggerton (Head of Store) and Mark Jones

English Heritage

Wolverhampton Express and Star

Professor Carl Chinn

Catherine Simpson

Barbara Handley

Christine Wright

Preface

MY NOTES jotted down about memories of my years of childhood spent living in Wolverhampton town centre were looked at by the then Rector of St Peter's Collegiate Church, Reverend John Hall Matthews. He thought these notes were worth putting into a small booklet, as a fund-raiser for the church. It was entitled "Under the Wing of St Peter's" and was produced in the Church Office. It first became available in 1995, the year after St Peter's had celebrated a thousand years since its first known Charter granted by the Lady Wulfrun. This Charter came nine years after the Charter to Lady Wulfrun by King Aethelred.

I continued to make more notes as I recalled some of the things my parents and grandparents had told me about their lives, and Joyce and I did some research into our family history.

When Professor Carl Chinn asked if we would write some memories for him to use in his Thursday pages in the Express and Star, we began to put these notes into order. A section about living in Red Lion Street and being at Red Cross Street School appeared in Carl Chinn's Feature on two consecutive Thursdays in July 2007.

People, ordinary people, believe they have led ordinary lives, and have an ordinary family history. But everyone's story is of interest, and should be recorded while they can still remember, and while they still have older family members, or friends, whom they can ask for their own part of the story. Otherwise, once they are gone, their story, in the way only they can tell it, is lost for good.

Anthony Perry

Introduction

FROM the age of three or four, until I was eleven years old, we lived in Red Lion Street, in the centre of Wolverhampton. Memories of these years, in the 1950s, are certain to be hazy in some respects, but, from what I can recall, they are fond memories. Family, friends and the town centre, before it was to undergo such drastic alterations, combined to give a happy early childhood. Living where we did, it might be said we were under the shadow of St Peter's Collegiate Church, the grand Parish Church of Wolverhampton, standing on the highest point in the centre, and watching over everyone and everything until the advent of high-rise buildings. However, "under the shadow of" sounds a little ominous, especially with the role this church played in my upbringing. The phrase "under the wing of" is more appropriate.

I had been born at 146 Pinfold Lane, Penn, Wolverhampton, on 18 June 1951, or so I was told. My memory does not reach back that far, and, being unable to take notes at the time, I rely on my birth certificate. The house, now a much-altered three bedroomed semi-detached, was the home of my maternal grandmother and her second husband, Francis Weetman, my step-grandfather. From the time I could utter any sort of words, "Granddad" was too difficult to pronounce, he became "Gaga" and this affectionate name stuck.

They had moved into the house when it was built in 1935, and when Pinfold Lane was still a country lane. It had not been widened into the suburban through route it is now, but the deeds of the houses built during that period provided for the Council taking part of the front garden away to allow for the road widening to take place. My grandmother had moved in, but as they had not yet married, Frank was still living at home with elderly parents.

1.

The Family Background of the Amphletts

MY GRANDMOTHER, Nora Gwendoline, was born an Amphlett, a name still common in parts of the Midlands. The Society of those who have the name or are associated with it calls the Amphletts "the River People" – around the Vale of the Severn. Nora was one of ten children born to William and Ellen Amphlett at Mill Cottage, one of a pair of semi-detached cottages adjacent to and belonging to Mill Farm, with its attractive Georgian Farmhouse, on the main Gloucester Road in the straggling village of Castlemorton in Worcestershire, near to its border with Gloucestershire and Herefordshire and overlooked by the Malvern Hills.

Ellen's maiden name was Lloyd Lawley, and she had been born around 1871 at the tiny village of Woolaston, between Chepstow and Lydney in Gloucestershire. Her parents were William, a cordweiner or bootmaker who had originated from Dudley, and Mary Ann, who came from Whitebrook, Gwent, only a few miles from Woolaston on the banks of the River Wye. Mary Ann was 14 years younger than William, being already about 36 when Ellen was born, whilst William was near enough 50. By 1881 they were living not far away from Castlemorton, at Hook Common to the west of Upton-upon-Severn.

William Amphlett was also born around 1871, to George and Emily Amphlett. George, a labourer, had not moved far, having originated from the village of Twyning, just across the River Severn. In 1881 the family, which included an older sister to William, Rose, and a younger one, Prisilay, were

Mill Farm, on the main road in Castlemorton, for whom William Amphlett worked. (Photograph Joyce Perry)

living at Drakes Street in the village of Welland. By this time, George's mother, who also came from Twyning, was a widow. She was living in one of the numerous closely packed alleyways in the town of Tewkesbury, Glover's Alley. Out of 90 alleys which may have existed, only 30 survive, and sadly Glover's Alley was a victim of the need in the 1960s to sweep away old buildings and replace them with modern shops, at the northern end of the High Street.

George's parents were George Smith and Jane Amphlett who had never married and George kept his mother's name. Not long after George was born Jane married John Green and they started a family. In the census George's name appears as Green and presumably this was so that he did not appear to have been illegitimate. However, after George married Emily and they had a couple of children their name appeared as Hamblin, but through the years it was eventually spelt correctly as Amphlett.

William was a farm labourer like his father, when he and Ellen married on 5 November 1892 at the three-storey grand Wesleyan Chapel at the Home

End in Ledbury. The story behind them having ten children was told that, when he came home from a drink at the pub, if he hung his trousers on the bedpost Ellen knew another baby was on the way. Mill Cottage was not large so there was a lot of sharing of bedroom space. William served as a Private in the Royal London Fusiliers in the Great War, and they lived much of their lives in the Malvern area. Nora's brothers and sisters were Ellen, known as Nell, Elsie May, Edith Marguerita, known as Peggy, Alice who died young in the 1920s of leukaemia, Albert Edward, Alfred John, Arthur George, Hubert James and William Henry.

Nora was the second oldest of the ten and would take on some of the responsibility for the younger ones. There was no school in Castlemorton to begin with, and they therefore walked over two miles to the nearest school in the village of Welland. Being in an agricultural community, children would be expected to help with some of the work on the farm, in addition to household jobs, and hopefully having enough time left over to learn from their school lessons. It was not unusual for children to be missing from school if there was something urgent to be done, particularly around harvest time. Paid

Mill Cottage, attached to Mill Farm, where William and Ellen Amphlett brought up their large family. (Photograph Joyce Perry)

employment was difficult to obtain locally, probably not helped by being in a large family, so Nora and several of her brothers and sisters worked in service from a young age. There were many large houses and families in need of domestic staff. Others worked on the land, for one or other of the large estates, or for the Great Western Railway. Arthur became Foreman of Great Malvern Station. But essentially they were country children, who learned from experience about picking wild fruit, what could be eaten and what could not, helping with harvesting, milking, collecting eggs, that the pig you talk to has to die some day if you want bacon. They would walk to most places, unless there was a chance of a ride on a cart. Their knowledge of the birds and bees was gained through a "fern ticket" on the Malvern Hills. In later years some of them might never feel at home, having been forced through circumstances to change to an urban environment; and they would easily hark back to quieter, simpler times.

2.

The Averill Family

NORA married William Averill on 30 May 1918 at Christchurch in Malvern. He was from the nearby village of Bromsberrow Heath, not far from Castlemorton, and was aged 25, having been born on 22 January 1893. Before the Great War he had seen service with the Royal Navy, having joined on 8 September 1911. You used to hear of men who had "run away to sea", and William was one young man who did this, to get away from his father, Samuel Averill.

Samuel's wife Emma was 9 years younger than him, and they had a large family – William, Thomas, George, Charlotte, Kate, Harriet, Anne, Lucy or Mary, and Samuel. Charlotte was known as Lottie, and her son Clifford emigrated to New Zealand and married an Australian girl, Alma. Kate was the only one of that generation I remember. Kate married engine driver Edward Dobbs, who drove steam locomotives on the Central Wales or Heart of Wales Line, a scenic route from Shrewsbury to Swansea which still operates today. Kate and Ted lived in a terraced house in the centre of Swansea, not far from the old Victoria Station, which was the terminus of the southern section of the line, until this was closed and services were transferred to High Street Station. He would drive as far as the half-way point, the Sugarloaf tunnel and summit, a lonely spot, where he and his fireman might find themselves having to leave their warm cab on a freezing winter night to deal with the iced up rails, and where the line clings to the sides of the steep valley at the southern end of the tunnel. Their original house was destroyed by German bombing during the Second World War, as were so many in Swansea, which suffered a lot from enemy action. They moved to another terraced house nearby in Plymouth Street, which was to be part of a clearance scheme many years later to make way for a new bus station. Auntie Kate's stories of Ted included her most embarrassing moment one day when she was shopping in the town's Woolworth's store. He must have got fed up of waiting at one of the entrance doors for her, and his loud voice bellowing "Kite!" could be heard throughout the store. She pretended not to know him and left the shop without him by another exit!

William and Nora Averill stand next to her parents Ellen and William Amphlett in the front garden of their house in Malvern taken about 1920.

Thomas joined the First Battalion, the Herefordshire Regiment, died of wounds sustained in battle in November 1918, and is buried at Terlincthun Cemetery, Wimiville in France.

George was a married man and father of 2 children when he joined up at Gloucester in 1916. He became a Roller Driver with 315 Road Construction Company, and this was an occupation he continued in civilian life.

The father, Samuel, had been born at Dymock in 1844, and was a gamekeeper before becoming a farm labourer and then a shepherd at Bromsberrow. His wife Emma was born at Kempsey in 1854. Samuel's parents were George Averill, born 1820 and Charlotte Chinn, born 1819, both from Dymock, and they were married in 1843. They lived in the Dymock area all their lives, where George was a farmer. George's father Samuel, born about 1791, had originated from Newnham, several miles south on the River Severn, from where he moved to Dymock and married Harriet, born in the village about 1793. George was Innkeeper at the Plough and later also farmed land there.

So William had left the comfort of brothers and sisters, and probably a loving mother, because of a difficult father. When the Great War began, he became a First Class Stoker on HMS Tiger and took part in the Battles of Jutland in May 1916, when 24 of the crew were killed and 46 wounded, and Dogger Bank in January 1915, when 10 crew were killed. He received 4 medals while on active service. Although he left the Navy when the war finished, he continued to be on Reserve, eventually being discharged on 25 July 1927. When my mother Phyllis Gwendoline was born on 3 March 1919, at 1 Sherrard's Green Cottage, Guarlford, near Malvern, he was still recorded on the certificate as being a First Class Stoker in the Royal Navy.

William Averill in the uniform of HMS Tiger taken during the First World War.

Whilst William, who was known as Bill, survived the Great War, others from his home village were not so fortunate. The impressive War Memorial in Bromsberrow rededicated in 2011, records that 12 men from the Parish lost their lives, including Thomas Averill.

Phyllis' brother, my uncle Ken, was born a few years later, and Bill Averill brought his family to Wolverhampton, for a job as a gas stoker at Stafford

Road Gas Works. They took the tenancy of a house just a short walk from his employment at 56 West Street, one of a few streets of terraced houses which climbed up from Stafford Road to Dunstall Hill, all of which have long since been redeveloped with retail warehouses.

Phyllis and Ken as youngsters were at the same infant and junior schools as I was to go to – Red Cross Street. This was a Victorian school, one of the original Board Schools, which opened in 1873 with a Department for boys, one for girls and another for infants. This stood roughly where the Asda Supermarket is now. It had frontages to Red Cross Street and Birchfield Street, two of a series of streets which joined the old North Street to Molineux Street, where the walls of the old Molineux Street stand of the Wolves' Football Ground came right up to the back of pavement. The boys' and girls' Departments came together in 1931 to be a mixed Junior School, and in 1936 a new building was created for the infants. The infants' school had a veranda with five classrooms opening into it and facing a playground with a "Jungle Jim" frame for climbing. The Assembly Hall, in an Art Deco style, had large round-headed windows which reached to the wood-block floor to give maximum light. The older junior school had classrooms around a courtyard playground, again with a glazed veranda to protect children going between rooms, an extra playground area where boys would play football, and a third piece at the back of the buildings fronting Red Cross Street. There was a large high hall used for assembly and gym. Perhaps it had been at one time divided up by screens into separate classrooms, to judge from the construction, with its pillars and roof beams. One quarter of the hall had a wooden platform or stage, with the wooden frame of what could have been a proscenium arch, but there were no curtains, scenery, backdrop or lighting frame.

When they reached the age of 11 there was a change in schools for Phyllis and Ken, with the family's first contact with St Peter's Church. Despite them having an association with the Baptist Church which used to be at Waterloo Road, they moved to St Peter's Collegiate Secondary Schools, also late Victorian buildings, in St Peter's Square, where the Wolverhampton University modern entrance block is now. This was built partly on the second St Peter's churchyard, behind the College of Technology, which is now the main entrance block of the University, with its "Marble" hall. This College had in the 1920s replaced the 17th Century Deanery House, despite a public outcry against its loss because it was believed to have been designed by Christopher Wren, whose father and uncle had been Deans of

Wolverhampton and Windsor. The only concession made was to save panelling from the Deanery and fit it in the College Principal's room.

The first St Peter's Churchyard was of course the area immediately surrounding the Church, where the remains in the graves were left but the headstones removed to enable St Peter's Gardens to be laid out in the 1930s. The playground of St Peter's Schools still had upright headstones lining its outer edge.

Phyllis looked after her younger brother, and had to defend him in the occasional scrape. When she was caught defending herself against some bully who had been plaguing her for some time, she was taken to the headmistress. She was asked why she had been fighting. "My father has brought me up to stand up for myself," she answered. The head's response was: "I try to bring up my girls to be young ladies." Mum never told me what happened to the bully, so I suppose she escaped punishment, as they often do. But I understand Mum had some sort of revenge later without being caught!

The job at the gas works was to have a deteriorating effect on Bill's health, which had not been left good through the conditions he had worked in during the War. In 1933 he was taken into hospital with a problem with his stomach. Surgeons opened him up to discover cancer in his liver so far developed there was nothing to be done, and with so little time left he was not even sewn up properly. At the age of 14 Phyllis was too young to be allowed into the ward to see him. But with a strong–willed determination she managed to quietly climb a wall, and enter through an open window. Once inside, she announced to the Ward Sister standing in her way that nothing would stop her seeing her father. She was allowed to be with him for just a few minutes. At her vulnerable age the loss of her father made a deep impression on Phyllis, and the sadness and resentment was always just below the surface, even 50 years later.

Her brother Ken was only 9 years old, and was not able to go with her. He was most upset by this, and also upset at not being allowed to go to his father's funeral – children simply were not taken. The strain and confusion stayed with him for the rest of his life. He did not want to go to hospital for treatment for sickness or check-ups, nor did he want members of his family to go. He always said hospitals were for the dying, and once you went in you did not come out. He also found it hard to attend funerals, even though he had a great Christian faith.

3.

Hard Times

LIFE was hard for Nora and her two children, particularly before her widow's pension was available. A visit from a welfare officer resulted in the person being shown the door unceremoniously, after the suggestion Nora should sell their second-hand upright piano on which the children were learning to play. Someone told Nora she should go to the Royal British Legion for help, in view of Bill's service in the Navy during the War. On a winter's day she sat patiently waiting for what seemed like an age in a freezing anteroom and almost passed out. She was eventually shown into a room with a roaring fire and two gentlemen who were presumably some kind of assessors. They listened to her story and replied: "We do not help sailors' wives." Nora's comment as she left them was: "If that's charity you can keep it." She did not seek further help. From that day the family would never buy a poppy for Remembrance Sunday.

The first time I recall coming home and thinking I had done the right thing by saying I had put some money into a collecting box, and wearing a poppy, my mother was still upset at relating this incident. I have never felt able to buy a poppy again since then. The Royal British Legion is more sympathetic and considerate these days.

They had a dog, Pip, who would walk quite a distance from West Street to Wolverhampton Retail Market, almost a mile, and although the road traffic was small by today's standards the journey still included crossing busy streets. Perhaps Pip was known by one or more of the butchers, because he would return with a bone. One day he came home with a chop between his teeth. Nora took it from him and declared: "There you are. We'll wash that – it's our dinner for today!" She washed it, cooked it and divided it so they each had a meal with a little meat on that day.

Nora's mother, Ellen, came to Wolverhampton from Malvern, I believe as a result of Phyllis' writing to her grandmother with a plea that they could not cope, as Nora was too proud to ask for help. Ellen's shock at the desperate plight of her daughter and grandchildren was short-lived, as she was a practical person. She had brought some food with her, and set to work in helping them. Nora asked why she had come, and scolded Phyllis for having written to her grandmother.

The financial situation meant that Nora had to take in washing and do other jobs she could find, which did not make it always possible for her to be at home. Her previous experience in domestic service was good background for her taking on the role of part-time housekeeper – in reality she did housework and whatever else might be needed on certain days of the week – for Mr and Mrs Dobbs. They lived in a detached house in Coalway Road, Penn, opposite Beckminster Road. Mrs Katherine Dobbs had been born a Hall, one of the family whose firm Alfred Hall and Sons had run a traditional and quality gentlemen's outfitters in Queen Square, Wolverhampton. This job developed into more of a friendship, so that Nora would help with looking after Mrs Dobbs' daughter Marna while she was out. It was to last long after the death of Mr Dobbs, and Marna had married and had children of her own. I think Nora was still doing a morning a week when she was in her 70s and until not long before Mrs Dobbs died. The family's kindness extended to gifts to help Nora out, and we still have a couple of items of furniture which came in that way.

Joining a "club" of some kind was necessary in those days to buy things you could not afford to pay for in a lump sum. The National Clothing and Supply Company was one such organisation, and they had links with a number of shops in the town. You would obtain a cheque from your National agent for whatever you wanted to buy, and this would appear as a debit in your National record book. The cheque would be produced at the appropriate shop in exchange for the goods. Your agent would then call at the house to collect regular payments until you were paid up. Nora's agent was Francis Weetman, with whom she struck up a friendship.

4.

The Weetman Family

THE WEETMAN family lived in a semi-terraced house in Bromley Street, off Dudley Road, Blakenhall, Wolverhampton, having originated in Cannock, where the name survives – perhaps there are distant relatives there. Frank's father and mother had moved to Wolverhampton after their first three children were born – Frank and his twin sister Dorothy, who was known as Dolly, in 1899, in Walsall Road, Cannock, and Gwen. They then had another daughter, Phyllis, born in 1908, and another son, Stanley, who only survived to the age of fourteen months, and was buried in a small grave at Sedgley Churchyard.

The Weetmans' house was just across the street from St Luke's Church and Primary School. Frank was a poor riser as a lad, and he could use the school bell as the signal to run across the street into school without being counted as being late. His first job on leaving school at the age of thirteen years and nine months was at Holcroft's Works, Ettingshall. At sixteen he lied about his age and joined up to fight in the Great War, to the dismay and upset of his family. His battalion, the First Leicestershire, saw action in France, including the Battle at Verdun, but he would never talk about the fighting, except to say that, although the Germans were the enemy, he thought more of them as soldiers than he did the French. However, he would overcome the emotion to explain how he came by a little silver crucifix. When they were marching through Lille, a little girl, less than ten years old, broke away from the crowd lining the street and went to him. She broke the crucifix off her rosary and gave it to him. He put it in his pocket and when he came home on leave he brought it with him to give to his mother. She insisted he should keep it and carry it with him, as it would bring him back safely when the War was over. He came back without having been injured. We still have the little girl's crucifix, Frank's Victory and British medals, his Leicestershire Regiment badge and the shamrock he wore on his uniform.

Dolly went into nursing and ended up as the matron in charge of Bridge Home, an institution for men with learning difficulties, at Witham, Essex. She died tragically through drowning in the bath when I was quite young. She and her twin brother were quite alike in appearance. Gwen married an Edgar Wellington and brought up a family in Hereford.

Frank Weetman by the family house in Bromley Street, Blakenhall, about 1920.

Phyllis worked in service for some years, and had posts in fairly well-to-do families in Wolverhampton, including Graiseley Old Hall, and also in London, where one job saw her take the unusual role of a gentleman's valet. So she learned about domestic matters, the kitchen and housekeeping, but she also had to learn about the attire and accessories of a gentleman – suits for different occasions, how to lay things out for him, the care of his clothing, and making sure everything was just so. She moved into the Health Service, and trained as an occupational therapist. She worked with sister Dolly until the latter's untimely passing, then spent the remaining years of her working life at St George's Hospital, Stafford, where she referred to her patients with learning difficulties as "my boys".

5.

The Need to Break Away

SO Frank and Nora had started going out together, not many months after Nora losing her husband Bill so tragically. The lack of sufficient grieving time in the hearts and minds of Phyllis and Ken, who had lost a loving father at impressionable ages, led to conflict with Frank. Phyllis did not find out until years later how badly Ken took the loss, because he kept it all to himself. She herself felt a sense of rejection, and could not accept this new man in her mother's life. She sought solace at her grandparents' home in Malvern.

However, she must have ventured to explore the new family with whom they had become associated, because she found Frank's mother and father to be very kind and welcoming. Perhaps they were the means for her to move a little way towards accepting that her mother was going to re-marry.

Phyllis was fourteen when she left school and started to find employment at various shops in Wolverhampton Town Centre. One of her first jobs was surely the shortest lasting – one day – at a bakery and cake shop. When she was told at the end of the day she had to scrub the floor of the

The first James Beattie, remembered by Phyllis Averill when working at Beatties' Department Store as a teenager. (Photograph Joyce Perry, courtesy Beatties Department Store, House of Fraser)

shop before she could go home, she told them what they could do with the floor. Another job was at Hill's and Steele's, which became British Home Stores, and she made some friends there.

She also worked for some time at James Beattie's Department Store. This had begun life as the Victoria Drapery, a small shop in Victoria Street, Wolverhampton, opened in 1877 by the first James Beattie. It expanded into a department store over the next fifty years by taking over adjoining buildings, rebuilding and re-fronting as the business became more and more successful. So when you walk through the store and go up and down a few steps in different places, you are merely entering what had been another building. For instance, the section of the Victoria Street frontage which on the ground floor contains greeting cards, stationery, haberdashery and so on, several steps lower than the adjoining parts of the store, started off life as the Villiers Club, and was converted in 1911 to become the Picture House cinema, to take advantage of the growing new craze, showing silent films. It was sold to Beatties in 1926, but they continued its use as a cinema until 1929, when the Council's plans to widen Victoria Street by a few feet led to Beatties' design for its grand Art Deco frontage. This included for the building at the lower end, the cinema, being set back in an arc, as the upper floors still are, and my mother said that at the centre of the arc was the entrance to an arcade that went through the store, to Townwell Fold at the rear. If you go up the stairs from the greeting cards and look through the windows you can see what was the roof of the Picture House. Bits of its ceiling plasterwork are thought to be hidden above the false ceiling of the ground floor.

James Beattie's first shop, Victoria Drapery, in Victoria Street, opened 1877. (Photograph Joyce Perry, courtesy Beatties Department Store, House of Fraser)

The part of the frontage which is at the Queen Square corner was built in 1932 for gentlemen's outfitter's Montague Burton, another Art Deco type of design with its stylised elephants' heads between the upper floor windows.

Beatties' Art Deco 1929 frontage to Victoria Street, showing the arc, at the middle of which began an arcade through the store. (Photograph Joyce Perry, courtesy Beatties' Department Store, House of Fraser)

James Beattie's 21st Birthday Party with the Store Staff. Phyllis Averill is third from the left in the front row of those standing. (Photograph courtesy Beatties Department Store, House of Fraser)

Kenneth Perry, on one knee in his sailor suit, is in the centre of this photograph of an All Saints' School Maypole Dance, dating from the early 1920s.

Beatties purchased the freehold of this from the Council and the leasehold interest from Burton's.

From her early days working there, Phyllis remembered the first Mr Beattie, an "old father time" figure who still came into the store regularly in his old age and knew and found time to speak to the young girls at the counters. She worked and trained on different department counters, such as hosiery, but for part of her period of employment there Phyllis was a uniformed lift operator, so she would see the three generations of the family often. The first James Beattie was well liked, his son was not. She remembered how he used to breathe whiskey over her in the lift. The grandson James Beattie, who took over from his father, died in 1987, was well liked by the staff. Presumably he inherited his character from his grandfather and not his father. He threw a party for the staff to celebrate his twenty-first birthday and a commemorative photograph of this happy occasion shows Phyllis amongst the people there.

In the 1930s shopgirls were treated in different ways by different shopkeepers, store owners or managers. Whether the first James Beattie was a good example, he was a true 'Victorian' entrepreneur, who may have employed girls from the early days of his store. By the time he was in his 80s, he appreciated the value of the quality, hard work and loyalty of the ladies, and they appreciated him. They may have had to work long hours, such as having to stay late after shop hours to prepare for sales beginning the following morning, but that probably continues today.

Phyllis was an ardent socialist, although she too appreciated the care for the staff by the bosses. What she did not appreciate, and would have had to bite her lip, was that, although Beatties was intended as a store for all Wolverhampton and surrounding area to use and enjoy, some of those from the 'posh' parts of the town would treat shopgirls in a condescending way, as if they were servants. For instance a lady might come in to buy relatively small items, such as a pair of stockings, but would delight in telling the shop assistant to have them delivered, rather than carrying them! Phyllis was asked to make a delivery of this sort, two or three miles out of town, and had to walk, not being given the bus fare. When she arrived at the house and was greeted at the front door by a servant of some kind, who said that the tradesmen's entrance was at the rear, she pushed the package into the hands of the startled servant, saying that after walking all that way they could have the package then and there or not at all!

The second James Beattie, grandson of the first. (Photograph Joyce Perry, courtesy Beatties Department Store, House of Fraser)

Phyllis went out socially with a few girl friends. One evening they met up with a group of young men, amongst whom she met a certain Kenneth Perry, who asked her out for a date. Ken was the only child of Henry John and Jane Perry. Jane, née Pearson, was affectionately known as Jinny, Henry as Harry. Ken was born on 20 July 1917, and so was two years older than Phyllis, and the family lived in a terraced house, No 72 Granville Street, in the All Saints district of Wolverhampton. Ken had also been a pupil at St Peter's Secondary School, following his time at All Saints' Infants and Juniors.

His father, Harry, had been born in Wolverhampton on 20 April 1889, one of a large family of brothers and sisters, whose parents were John Samuel and Sarah Perry. John had married Sarah Carter on 14 October 1888 at St Paul's

Church, which was just off Penn Road next to the Sunbeamland building, and was sadly demolished when Penn Road was made into a dual carriage-way. At the time they were both living at Graiseley Row, just round the corner from the Church, and John was a locksmith. His father, also named John Samuel, was already dead. Records show he had been born on 12 November 1863 at "California", Wolverhampton. Whilst we have come across the "Caribbee Island" being the nickname for the streets off Stafford Street, we have yet to discover where "California" was, and would be pleased to hear from any readers who can identify the location. The family seems to have come from Walsall, but this trail could not be followed. Sarah, a machinist, was daughter to another locksmith, Charles Carter.

Of Harry's brothers and sisters, I recall meeting Alice, Ella, Nancy, Arthur and Stan. I remember Ella had a cleft palate, which made it a little difficult to understand her speech. She had been in domestic service in her younger life. She was already retired when I met her, at first living in a house near to West Park, then moving to a multi-storey block of flats at Evans Street, Whitmore Reans, Wolverhampton. We visited her in hospital after she had been knocked down in an accident.

Arthur married a lady we knew as Aunt Nell, and they had a daughter, Linda. Stan had similar looks to Harry, and I did not know his family, except for meeting his wife a few times in later years. There was another brother, Frank, who had perhaps died before I was born. Another brother, Edward, known as Ted, moved to Swindon and was a footballer, playing in goal, and an athlete, then in later years he was involved in the more sedate sport of bowls.

John and Sarah Perry with two of their children, in the early 1890s. Harry likely to be the one on the left.

Jane Pearson had been born on 19 September 1883 to Edward and Mary Ann Pearson, who came from Bradley, Edward being an iron puddler. Edward and Mary Ann had five children in addition to Jane. First, there was George who married Clara, and their children were George, Marjorie, Lilian and another. Secondly there was Leonard who married Ada Cross, and their two daughters were Maisie and

A Frank Pearson photograph of Phyllis in the late 1930s.

Joan, who became the wife of Carol Valasek, from Eastern Europe, who had worked at a Wolverhampton car sales business called Carol's Motors at the town end of Penn Road, which grew and changed out of all recognition. Third, there was Albert, who married Louisa Hotchkiss, and they had a son, Albert, and daughters Mary and Millicent. Millie, as she was always known, passed away in June 2010, and she helped greatly in piecing together the connections on the Pearson side of the family. She had been widowed for many years from her husband. They had four children, the oldest being John, the second oldest was Pam, whose first husband was Mervin Noakes, brother of Barry Noakes, who became a well-known and popular character at the Grand Theatre, running one of the Lounge Bars, occasionally appearing on stage, as well as doing some television work. Pam and Mervyn had two sons, Christopher and David. The third child was Michael and the fourth was Diane. Fourth child to Edward and Mary Ann Pearson was Marie, who had married and had two daughters, Constance, who married Jim Sparrow, and Jean, who married bus driver David Lewis. She remarried after divorcing him.

I recall when I was little being taken to see Auntie Jean and Uncle Dave at their bungalow, one of the pre-fabricated types off the main Willenhall Road from Wolverhampton. The "prefabs" were supposed to be a short term local authority solution to housing needs during the period after the Second World War, and intended to last for about ten years, but they were quite popular, in effect being detached bungalows. Many of these were demolished, but some remain in Wolverhampton, at Bushbury and Henwood Road, Compton, where they were encased in brick some years ago. Jean and Dave's children were Ian and his sisters Wendy and Tina, and as Ian was of a similar age to me, I had hopes of a friendship with this cousin. We did spend some time together, and I remember one incident, when Ian was staying with us and my mother took us for an outing to Tettenhall Upper Green Pool. Ian lost his footing and fell into the pool. After the initial shock, and, finding to his relief that it was only inches deep and not feet, he discovered the only damage was the odd minor cut and some bruising. But it resulted in Mum having to patch him up and kit him out with dry clothes from a local shop. I suppose the reason the friendship did not continue was that we did not live close to each other.

The fifth other Pearson child was Frank, who was disabled with a back deformity. He was recalled by my parents as being a very good amateur photographer who loved taking portrait and other photographs, adding his own colour to some of them. He took a lovely portrait of Phyllis, and some interesting pictures of buildings, including interior shots of Churches, including All Saints.

My grandfather Henry Perry was reputed to have played football for West Bromwich Albion before the First World War, but so far we have been unable to find anyone with records to confirm this – perhaps he did not make the first team. We have a lovely portrait taken of him and Jane, we think at the time of their wedding, and separate large portraits of each of them at the same time. As far as we can tell from records he served with the Wiltshire Regiment in the Great War as a Colour Sergeant.

Harry's work was in engineering, and he was recorded on documents as a fitter. Although I never heard tell that he rode a motorcycle as a regular thing, he was employed as a mechanic and fitter by more than one of the once famous local manufacturers, such as AJS, Villiers and Sunbeam, whose factories were just a stone's throw away from Graiseley Row. This employment gave him the opportunity to travel with the motorcycle teams to the Isle of Man on the occasion of the TT races, to look after the machines. In his later working life he moved within the engineering industry to larger machines and was employed as a fitter at factories making aircraft parts, such as Hobsons, who were at Fordhouses, Wolverhampton.

Harry Perry is in the centre of the front row in this unidentified football team photograph taken about 1910.

Harry Perry is third from the left on the back row in an unidentified works team picture, taken about 1920s.

6.

Living at All Saints

K EN had failed the medical examination for entry into the forces during the Second World War, and was therefore available for war work within industry. Phyllis also became involved in war work and was a progress chaser at the Boulton Paul aircraft factory at Pendeford, Wolverhampton, makers of the Defiant fighters. Being an attractive girl, she proved popular with the male office and factory workers, but she stayed with Ken and they were married on 29 April 1942 at St Philip's Church, Pennfields, Wolverhampton. To begin with they lived with Ken's parents at 72, Granville Street, then after the death of Mary Ann Pearson in August 1943 they were able to take her tenancy at 78 Dartmouth St, which was the next street in the All Saints district of Wolverhampton. These houses were owned by the same landlord, which is perhaps how they came to get the tenancy of the house. Both were typical two storey terraced houses, with no front garden. The front door opened straight into the parlour with the living room behind, off which were the steep stairs leading up to the two double and one single bedrooms. From the living room you would walk through to the back kitchen, and outside was a yard, paved with blue bricks, an outside toilet and a coalhouse. There was no rear garden but a right of way at the end of the yard which served four houses, with a tunnel entry between the two pairs of houses.

At Granville Street, Harry and Jane lived in the left hand house of a similar block of four. In the right hand house of the same block, and so sharing the same entry, lived Edgar and Violet Woodward, a homely couple, who had one daughter, Barbara. The Woodwards were helpful friends to the Perrys, and

Kenneth and Phyllis Perry sit on the front doorstep of 78 Dartmouth Street, All Saints with Tony, about 1954.

years later, probably for my benefit, they were referred to as Auntie Vi and Uncle Edgar. It was a time when friends of parents were often referred to as Auntie and Uncle.

Phyllis had already taken to her mother-in-law and would spend lots of time with her. Perhaps they found comfort from each other, as Ken and his father would like to go out regularly for a drink, to their nearest public house, The Dartmouth Arms, in Vicarage Road. This was just around the corner from both Granville Street and Dartmouth Street, and its public bar tended to be mainly populated by the menfolk of the neighbourhood. They would offer to take the ladies, who did not spend so much time and money in public houses and in any case the ladies' preference was the White Rose, a couple of streets away in Powlett Street. Here they were friendly with the people who kept the establishment, which had a pleasant family room and a garden at the back for use in fine weather.

If the social life of the menfolk centred around a pint glass, the ladies took solace at All Saints' Church, which had been built between 1877 and 1879 at Steelhouse Lane to replace the earlier Mission Church and serve the tightly knit community contained in the rows of terraced houses. It was a large church and the worship area is now much smaller, contained in what was the Chancel and Chapels, as the greater part of the building today forms a community centre. It does, however, contain some important features, including the beautiful reredos, designed by Sir Charles Nicholson, and the spectacular paintings either side by Charles' younger brother Archibald Nicholson. The Victorian All Saints' School was attached, and at the rear, using up what space was available, there was built a hall for classes, functions and meetings. The funds to build this Hall had been raised by the Minister, Father Ensor, who was loved by his congregation as much for his care and concern of his parishioners as for his ability as a minister and his spirituality. The Hall was used by the Mothers' Union for their meetings, and Phyllis and Jane Perry and Vi Woodward were regulars at these, as well as for the outings to places of interest. The Hall was also used for dances, scout meetings, beetle drives, and fish and chip suppers.

7.

Frank Weetman

A VISIT to her own mother was a walk, or a bus ride into Town, and then
another bus ride, for Phyllis. How long the relationship with Frank
remained strained I do not know. Frank had a reasonably paid job,
in comparison with men in factories, as a collecting agent for the National
Clothing Supply Company, although the hours were unsociable. The
company took advantage of the need for people to buy things for which they
could not pay all in one go. They produced catalogues and had shops
participating in their schemes to offer their goods. Customers were able to
pay by instalments at the Company's office or to the collecting agent who
would call on them at home. It was necessary for Frank to aim at times when
people were likely to be in, for example in the evenings or after pay day. He
collected from districts within and beyond the boundaries of
Wolverhampton, from people who could be difficult, refuse to pay at all, or
pretend to be out. It must have been very tiring, and sometimes frustrating.
He did not drive, and so it was all buses and legwork. The Scotlands, Low Hill,
Wednesfield and Short Heath were areas I remember him mentioning, and
these were all on the opposite side of Wolverhampton from Pinfold Lane.

Amongst his experiences, there was the day he witnessed a cyclist slow
down as he reached the brow of a canal bridge in Willenhall and lift himself
off his saddle to break wind loudly. The man looked back with a laugh to a
crowd of amused locals, including a group of factory girls who had a fit of the
giggles.

One of his customers was to be avoided for his temper, especially when he
had downed a few drinks, and his wife told Frank to only call when her

husband was out. She had not yet told him that she was buying something through the National. One day Frank happened to call when the man was in, and in a particularly drunken state, and of course when he found out why Frank was there he went for him. The wife grabbed her husband's braces at the back and shouted: "Get out Mr Weetman, while I hold him back" as the braces stretched to their limit. Frank needed no second bidding and was off. The next time he called, the husband was in again but this time sober. "Mr Weetman, I am very sorry for the way I behaved to you last week," he said, "come and have a drink on me to show you how sorry I am." "No, thanks," replied Frank, "you'll only do it again." There was the occasional offer by a housewife to Frank to pay her instalment owing on goods not in cash but in kind, and he could see without difficulty that the lady might be wearing a dressing gown or something similar but with nothing underneath, but Frank would politely decline and make a quick exit.

Standing next to the "largest pink flowers in the world", Frank Weetman pulls a face for the camera, next to Kenneth Perry, behind Tony, Nora Weetman and Phyllis Weetman, in the porch of 146 Pinfold Lane, Penn, taken about 1962.

I can remember in later years that he was out calling on his customers all day Monday and Tuesday, much of Friday and quite a lot of Saturday, not arriving home until 10 o'clock at night. Wednesdays and Thursdays were his days off, except for Wednesday morning, when he would take his books and money for checking and signing off at the National office, which was on the first floor of a building in Powlett Street, off Snow Hill, Wolverhampton.

Frank had a hunger for knowledge and education. Having left school at a young age, and soon afterwards being caught up in the nightmare of the trenches, he must have determined to broaden his mind by his own efforts. There was a second-hand/antiquarian bookshop called Start's in one of the 18th Century shops in King Street, Wolverhampton, which he would visit often, and come away with books in all sorts of categories – fiction, poetry, essays, books on literature, nature, discovery, history and religion. Nora said she knew when he had bought another book, because on his return home he would go straight upstairs. Days afterwards she might notice and remark on a new book surfacing in the collection, to which he would reply that he had bought it ages ago.

He was not an openly religious man, but kept his faith to himself. It was manifest in his love of, and being absorbed by, God's creation, whether it was through a country walk, or becoming immersed in looking after his beloved garden at Pinfold Lane. Gardening was a self-taught occupation. Remember that they were the first in the house at Pinfold Lane so they had to start from scratch. At the front was a privet hedge, about three feet high, immaculately kept in a rounded shape, with a creosoted fence immediately in front of it. A small lawn, with a limited border for planting, was bounded at the front of the house with a neatly kept low box hedge and a hydrangea which bore "the largest pink flowers in the world". A party drive between Nos 146 and 144, just wide enough for a small car to drive down, led to a step up through a high wooden gate, part of a six foot close boarded fence which was also kept creosoted (I used to love the smell of creosote when he had repainted it), onto a patio of slabs, except of course that they were not called patios then. This had been laid at too high a level, so that it bridged the damp proof course on the back wall of the house and caused a problem with the dining room floor which was never fixed. They just left a hole in the floor which gave enough ventilation and very occasionally access for the odd mouse. The French Windows from the dining room opened onto this slabbed terrace, with flowerbeds which housed Rose of Sharon, London Pride and low ground cover plants, divided by some small steps down to a lower level, and this gave the opportunity for a rockery effect on the slope. Where a garage would have been if the level of the terrace had not been raised, was a wooden shed, also creosoted, of course, for garden tools and equipment, and a second larger set of slabbed steps down to a path along the right-hand boundary. A dark red Berberis and Flowering Currant stood on the left with Lilac trees giving pink and lilac blossoms on the right. The lawn was always immaculately cut with barely a trace of weed or clover, and the flowerbeds on each side usually held a few roses, tall

Michaelmas Daisies and a mix of other flowering shrubs and bedding. Beyond the lawn two holly trees grew tall, and a crazy-paved path led between them. The open bed of shrubs included Evening Primroses, which shone out in the dark, and a gate at the end opened on to allotments. Frank took on the tenancy of one of these, and here he grew mainly vegetables.

If reading was a way of developing knowledge and broadening the mind, Frank went a step further by writing himself, essentially for his own amusement, but also for anyone else who wanted to see and appreciate his efforts. During the Second World War he produced a diary, in several volumes of home made books. In these he described walks, nature, what was happening around him, and he included pieces from the newspaper by way of articles and pictures, as well as illustrating with his own pen and ink or pencil drawings. These drawings could be highly detailed and were well observed. You could always tell if he was in a bad mood because his drawings would be dark. This diary with newspaper pieces continued after the War, and so included the bad winter of 1947. As he continued to read, he also wrote about what he had read, in the form of extensive notes on books, and there are several assorted volumes of these. At the outbreak of the War he was above the call up age, but his contribution to the national need, which must have led to being permanently tired, was as a member of the night time fire watching team. I believe this meant a look out post from the roofs or top floors of higher buildings in the town centre.

Phyllis must have softened to him, or at least appreciated his self-taught knowledge. His walks – and he really did enjoy walking – always proved to be interesting and educational. Who else, apart from Frank, Nora and Phyllis, went on these expeditions into the nearby countryside, I do not know. Nora would have felt at home, having been brought up in the rural area covering the borders of Worcestershire, Herefordshire, and Gloucestershire, with the fresh air, the chance to see aspects of nature and probably contribute to the interest of the event from her own background knowledge. Frank was not afraid of longer walks either, having had experience with his own father, who was a part-time fisherman. Francis senior thought nothing of coming home from work, having a food bag packed, and setting off to walk during the dark of the night to a suitable place ready to fish at dawn. They walked as far as Norbury Junction, on the Shropshire Union Canal, a distance of some twenty miles. How did they manage without sleep, how tired would they have been on their return home, having to walk back the same distance?

8.

Kenneth and Gladys Averill

KEN AVERILL, Phyllis' brother, worked for the Co-operative Store after leaving school, as a grocery shop assistant, and through this position he learned to drive and obtained his driving licence, using this to become a delivery boy. He was always keen on messing with cars. He was still living at home in Pinfold Lane, Penn, with his mother and sister, in the house that Frank had begun to buy in advance of marrying Nora, and Ken was still bottling up his grief at losing his father, and the difficulty of accepting a new step-father.

Ken met Gladys Smith, who had been born on 27 April 1925, and lived in the All Saints district of Wolverhampton, just a stone's throw from All Saints' Church, with her parents and sister Doreen. Gladys also worked for the Co-op, in their main office. They met for the first time at the Co-op Sports Field one Saturday afternoon, when Gladys, then aged 16, was playing tennis with the girls and Ken was playing cricket with the boys. For fun some of the boys had taken Gladys' brand new bicycle and hidden it in a thick patch of nettles, so she could not reach it without being stung. Ken saw the lady in distress, picked her up and carried her through the nettles, so that she could reach the handle bars and wheel the cycle out without being stung. She was very grateful and impressed by this young man's kindness.

Ken joined the Royal Marines on 19 August 1942, and was stationed at Portsmouth. Whilst on leave about a year later, he and Gladys met a second time in the Co-op Sports Room, where people could play table tennis, darts and other games. He complained he did not hear any news about his friends and colleagues while he was away, and she offered to write to him. Through

Kenneth Averill in his taxi outside 146 Pinfold Lane in the late 1940s.

correspondence they grew to know each other well, and every leave Ken would take her to the theatre or cinema. He was assigned to Australia in 1944 on the ship Orion. He manned the guns while transporting 5000 army soldiers from the United Kingdom, to protect Australia from Japan. He was demobbed on 17 July 1946, after serving for 2 years in Jervis Bay, New South Wales. He drove Army trucks from the ships to Sydney and further north. He would have been supposed to go to Normandy, but had to have an ankle operation, and while he was in hospital his ship sank. After the War marines, navy and soldiers were brought back to the United Kingdom to be demobbed and return home. Ken and Gladys were free to resume their relationship, and became engaged at Christmas 1948.

On his return from service Ken was offered a job by the Co-op in their butchery department, which was a laugh because he was soft with animals and would no more kill an animal than fly. So he declined the offer and became a taxi driver in Wolverhampton. Many years later he said that cab drivers in the 1940s were just as fast and furious as they were 50 years on! He was not happy that there were so few jobs available after the War, and the Americans seemed to have taken them all – the British servicemen had been promised jobs on their return.

Ken and Gladys were married at St Phillip's Church in Pennfields, Wolverhampton, on 10 September 1949, and lived temporarily with Phyllis and Ken Perry. But Ken Averill had decided that England was not for him any more and convinced Gladys that they could do better for themselves in new surroundings. Australia was a land of opportunities, the call was strong for Ken, there were friends he had made there and they could emigrate under an assisted scheme. So, much to the sadness of Nora and Phyllis, they set off to start a new life on 10 January 1950, on the ship Georgic, as migrants. He said such was the feeling when he saw his mother and sister waving goodbye at the docks, Ken wanted to get off the ship, and asked Gladys to do so with him. They arrived in Sydney on 13 February 1950, and Ken became a warranty clerk for Ford.

Gladys' sister Doreen married Tom Pickard, also from All Saints, in 1946, and they too emigrated to Australia, setting sail in February 1952, and arriving in March. They already had one daughter by this time, Gail. The two couples lived not far from each other in Wollongong, New South Wales.

9.

A Struggle through Adversity

THE WALKS which Frank led with Phyllis and Nora continued after the Second World War was over, but the fresh air did not prevent Phyllis' health crisis. She contracted Tuberculosis, through contact with a work colleague, or so it was thought, and was packed off to Prestwood and Groundslow Sanatoriums, for the benefits of rest and fresh air. How long she was treated I do not know, but she was determined to regain her health. We have photographs showing that she made friends with fellow patients. Perhaps from the days of living at West Street, the family doctor for her, her mother and brother, had been Doctor Jones, whose surgery was in a three-storey early Victorian villa in Waterloo Road. He was a kind, fair but firm doctor, well liked by his genuine patients, and probably not liked by any malingerers.

Phyllis had her heart set on having a child, specifically a baby boy, but Doctor Jones would not permit this when she returned home from her treatment for Tuberculosis. There needed to be a lengthy period before he would declare her as being all clear to try for a baby.

In the autumn of 1950 it was confirmed that she was pregnant, at which she was overjoyed. Ken's reaction was less than enthusiastic and so she knew she had to do a lot for herself, and maybe that is why I was born at my grandparents' house in Pinfold Lane, Penn. Maybe it was because I was born there that Frank had such great affection for me, and I took the place of the son he never had. Then maybe because I took the place of the son Frank never had, was that my father did not spend a lot of time with me?

Whatever the underlying reasons and background, my father's mother, Jane, did have great affection for me. For my first few years we lived in the next street to her and my grandfather in the All Saints area – we in Dartmouth Street, they in Granville Street. When we visited them, in the corner of the living room, between the chimney breast and door which opened to the steep stairs, was a box of toys brought out for me to play with. When my father and grandfather were out at the Dartmouth Arms, at the top of the street in Vicarage Road, my grandmother would come to our house to sit with my mother. If the ladies had an evening out, it would be at the Mothers' Union group, at All Saints Church. Here they found great comfort from the Minister and other ladies in the group.

If the family were to go out for a drink, say in the early evening taking me with them, the White Rose, which used to stand in Powlett Street, was the destination. It had a Children's or Family Room at the back, with a garden for us to use if the weather was fine – really no more than a few seats and tables on rough grass surrounded by a brick wall.

We had a loyal and affectionate dog when we lived in Dartmouth Street – a crossbred brownish coloured collie called Rex. He was very good with children – certainly very good with me. We had no bathroom in the house, so the large tin bath would have to be brought into the living room and filled with hot water from the kitchen on bath night. There was also a hob over the living-room fire which was contained in a black-lead grate, which had to be fed from the coal-house in the backyard next to the outside toilet. The front room or parlour fire was rarely lit as this room was reserved for special occasions.

10.

A Trip to Australia

FRANK WEETMAN travelled many miles as Agent for the National Clothing Supply Company. Sometimes he would walk quite a lot, if there was no bus, or the bus was full and sailed past the stop. He was known to arrive home soaking wet well after 10 o'clock at night if he had been unable to catch a bus from Town.

Sitting upstairs in the bus he could enjoy a smoke, and he would like to be in one of the front seats, to get the best view. One day in late 1955 when sitting in his favourite place the bus was involved in an accident, and Frank was thrown against the front window. Nothing was broken but he was taken to hospital and treated. His main injury, apart from cuts and bruises, was to one of his legs which left him with some pain and discomfort from time to time. Whatever the reason for the accident, the Transport Undertaking compensated him with quite a considerable sum of money.

Frank was aware how saddened Nora had been by her son Ken and Gladys emigrating to Australia. By this time they had a very young daughter, Karen, and Gladys was expecting another child. They kept in touch regularly by airmail letters, and there was no telephone in the house at Pinfold Lane for them to speak. So perhaps it was no surprise that Frank offered to use his compensation money to pay for Nora to go to Australia and spend six months there.

I doubt there was any discussion about Nora flying. It was six weeks' passage by ship to Sydney, in January 1956, calling at various places on the way, and Nora was sea sick for a lot of the time. She was befriended by a couple on the ship and they would go about together when they disembarked anywhere. The husband had to pull Nora away from a young Italian boy in Naples who had spat at them and called out "dirty English pigs". She said that was fine thing to say when she had seen people squat in the street rather than use a toilet! I think Gibraltar and Aden were among the other places they called at, and one of the ports in India.

During her time in Wollongong, Nora saw the birth of her third grandchild, a boy they named Craig, on 22 May 1956. Ken and Gladys' first child, Karen, had been born on 8 August 1954. She met with family and friends who made her so welcome it was difficult to leave when the time came to return home.

11.

The Move to Red Lion Street

I WAS only three or four years old when we moved house and became Council tenants for the first time, and so it is difficult to remember much regarding this first part of my life. It was not quick or easy to get a Council house but our family was recorded on their waiting list. Perhaps my parents requested a tenancy somewhere within or close to the town centre, so that we should be within walking distance or a short bus ride away from my grandparents in Granville Street, and also All Saints Church where my mother had built up a circle of friends. Whatever the records said, the Council's Housing Department came back to us with the offer of the tenancy of number 2 Red Lion Street, to which we moved in 1955. It must have been around then, because I had already started going to Sunday School at All Saints, and was accompanied by Edgar and Violet Woodward's daughter Barbara. I would be brought to their house in Granville Street by my father, for me to be taken on to All Saints by Barbara. After we had moved to Red Lion Street, I was still taken to the Woodwards' house on a Sunday for Barbara to continue looking after me in this way for some time afterwards.

Red Lion Street in the 1950s was longer than it is these days. The southern end, opening out onto Darlington Street, was much as it is now as regards the buildings. The rear part of the Magistrates Court and other offices were the Fire Station, and looking through the arched entrance into the courtyard, the building at the far end was the town centre Police Station with cells. Where the 1960s Telephone Exchange extension stands there was a block of four houses, Nos 1 to 4, let to Council Tenants. At right angles to the road was another block of four, fronting on to an alley, with a cemetery for St Peter and

1935 Aerial view of the centre of Wolverhampton, showing, below St Peter's Church, the Victorian Market Hall and open market patch with, to the left, the Wholesale Market, St Peter's Institute and St Peter's Secondary Schools. Below the Market Hall are the buildings later demolished to make way for the Civic Hall, then, to the left, the Telephone Exchange, then numbers 1 to 4 Red Lion Street in front of the old Blue Coat School/Education Offices, then numbers 5 to 8 fronting Paternoster Row leading up to the Catholic Church of St Peter and St Paul, numbers 9 and 10 behind the Catholic Cemetery, then numbers 11 to 14 before the junction of Red Lion Street with Wadhams Hill. Waterloo Road runs along the bottom of the photograph. (Aero Pictorial photograph used with permission of English Heritage)

St Paul's Catholic Church on the other side of the alley. A pair of semi-detached houses was situated behind the cemetery. Although the entrance to the alley from the street was up a step, through an opening between low brick walls surmounted by railings, it led, as Paternoster Row, up the hill, with a few garages fronting on to it, giving vehicle access to North Street.

At the top of the hill was the playground entrance to the school of the Catholic Church on the left hand side, followed by the main entrance up a

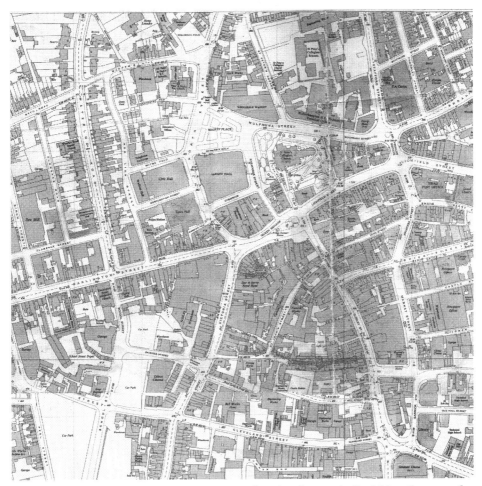

Part of early 1950s Ordnance Survey map showing houses in Red Lion Street and surrounding area.

flight of steps into the Church itself, which is still there now, with its prominent statues of St Peter and St Paul surveying the scene from the roof above the main entrance. On the right hand side were three houses, probably of similar age to the Church, about 1825, with rendered walls, and Georgian-type sash windows. Just beyond these was a car park which fronted on to North Street. Back down to Red Lion Street, which stretched a little further past the cemetery, with a final block of four houses before the junction with Wadham's Hill, where the Ring Road is now at a lower level. Nos 5 to 14 were let to police and fire officers.

The fourteen houses in the street were built in 1926, as shown by date plaques with the Wolverhampton Corporation Coat of Arms on the front walls. They were the typical between-the-Wars Council-built two-storey houses of brick and slate, with some rendering to the front walls on the first floor, bay windows to the ground floor front rooms, open porches and metal casement windows throughout. Unlike some Council houses of the period, our bathrooms were upstairs, along with three bedrooms, all large enough to take double beds, one of them of a size to accommodate a double and a single. This was mine for the first two or three years, as it had space for toys. I was moved into the front room over the porch and hall, a room in which I never felt easy, because sometimes I did not feel alone. It was as if I sensed something or someone within those four walls. One night when I turned over in bed I could make out a figure, a shape in the darkness standing over me, with eyes reflecting the outside lamplight. I screamed and dived beneath the bedclothes. When my parents came rushing in of course there was nothing there, but from that night I slept with the light on.

Downstairs were a kitchen with a coal store, an entrance hall with a pantry at the bottom of the stairs and two living rooms. The front one was fairly small with an ordinary fireplace, and was used very little – similar to how in our terraced house the front room was only used for special occasions. The rear room was larger, with a black-leaded grate. It was large enough to have a sideboard, dining table and chairs, plus a settee and easy chairs around the hearth rug. None of the houses had large gardens at front or rear, the middle six in the alley having no front at all, just a paved path running in front of the walls.

Our house was No 2 in the first block of four. A high privet hedge above a low brick wall along the back of pavement hid a small front garden where we grew, from time to time, Tulips, Daffodils and Nasturtiums. At the end of the tunnel entry you reached the backs of numbers 2 and 3, where the gardens were at a higher level than the yard areas by the back doors, and were held in by a retaining wall of large stones. These gardens were reached by steps, and the depth of the gardens was partly cut short by the back walls of some disused toilets, which had once served the former Bluecoat School, then used as Education Offices and a Clinic, in a large late Victorian building of dark red brick with overhanging gables. The entrance to this was from North Street. The building did not hold good memories, as it was here that children's teeth were extracted using gas, which always seemed to give nightmares while you were unconscious.

My best friend in these years was Geoffrey Leo. Although he lived at Wednesfield, his grandparents, Mr & Mrs Wythe, resided at No 3 –

neighbours who were very kind and friendly to my parents – and his mother or father would bring him from their house at Wednesfield to Red Lion Street regularly. The family's business was making and selling ice cream. Whilst his father came from an Italian family, his mother and her parents at No 3 were from East Anglia, and they had gentle Suffolk accents. We would spend many happy hours playing in each other's houses or in the street. My parents had no car and not a lot of money. I recall one day when Geoff and his family took me in their car to Milford Common, and treated me to ice cream. I had been given two sixpences and six pennies by my parents in case I needed anything. When we returned, I pushed what I thought was all of my money into Geoff's hand, asking him to give it to his father, towards petrol expenses. Not long after I had gone in the house, there was a knock at the front door. When my parents answered, it was Geoff, saying: "I think Tony must have dropped his pennies in the car." He held out the six pennies, and I discovered the two sixpences were still in my pocket. No comment on how I felt.

Other friends of ours in the street were John Hendley at No 5, who was replaced, when his family moved, by David Butcher, Sally Eades at No 6,

Next to the low wall and privet hedge at the front of Red Lion Street are Sally Edes, Geoffrey Leo, John Hendley and Tony, dating from around 1957.

replaced by a younger Sally Ormerod (I think Sally Eades was the first girl in whom I took an interest), Paul Makin at No 7, Lesley at No 10, Jane at No 12, Patrick Greatorex at No 13 (my next best friend after Geoff), and later on Jimmy and David Silcock at No 14. John at No 5, a life-long Wolves expert and supporter, was to become in later years a folk singer and successful co-ordinator of folk clubs in the area. Paul at No 7 became an actor, before realising the direction he wanted to take within the entertainment business and became a successful scriptwriter of television comedies, such as "A Kind of Living", "Nightingales", "Taking the Floor", "Grown Ups" and several episodes of "Goodnight Sweetheart". He was about two years younger than me, and sadly died of a brain tumour at the age of 54 in July 2008. Patrick at No 13 ran a popular hardware business in Wolverhampton.

The gang could vary in size from day to day, depending on who was available. In the 1950s playing in the street was second nature, with no fear of strangers, and we had the imagination to make up any number of different games, pretend dramas and shows, mimicking the stars seen on television or in films. The raised back garden of No 3 might be a stage, with Geoff's younger brother John using the inside part of a punch-ball as a microphone, belting out Frank Ifield's "I Remember You".

Play would often take place in the alley, and occasionally stray over the wall into the Catholic Cemetery. However, any parents hearing us would order us out, with the dire threat that we would "catch the fever" in there. No one ever explained what fever, and how it could be caught. It may be I took the threat more seriously, as I usually took some coaxing by the others to go over the wall. But it was worth a telling off, as it was another world in there – a wilderness of overgrown trees and bushes hiding old gravestones – certainly a good place for adventure. Occasionally we would play ball games in the alley, until the ball should happen to hit someone's door or window, and resulted in another telling off, or it disappeared through the gap in the railings at the bottom and on to the road in front of a passing car, to the annoyance of the driver! But the street was reasonably quiet for being so close to the town centre – used by motorists to park without using a car park.

Wadham's Hill was a street which could be busy, as it met Waterloo Road at a crossroads with traffic lights, and the route down Bath Road led to Chapel Ash. Hence it was a good route for traffic to miss the town centre. Waterloo Road was full of elegant Regency or early Victorian houses, in one of which was our doctor, the elderly, stern-looking but benevolent Doctor Jones, who

Red Lion Street in the 1950s. Number 2 is the second house to the left of the Telephone Exchange. (Courtesy Wolverhampton Archives and Local Studies)

had taken such great medical care of my mother during her long period of serious illness before I was born. He was held in high esteem. Bath Road was quite smart too, tree-lined with Victorian three-storey villas – many of the trees were left when the Ring Road was constructed, so the line of the road can still be detected – and the Welsh Church where the slope ended, followed by the Queen Victoria Nursing Institution. Wadham's Hill had more modest terraced houses, except for the large Gothic-horror-looking property at the corner of Whitmore Hill. On the right hand side, going up, was a house with a garden where we might be allowed in for our own bonfire on 5th November, then next to this was a groceries' warehouse of the Kidsons' Company. At the top of Wadham's Hill was Molineux Hotel, with a row of early houses to the right, known as Molineux Fold, fronting an open parking area. To the left Molineux Alley ran downhill past some derelict buildings. My step-grandfather, Frank, would take me past these sometimes so that we could look for the strange people he explained lived there, called the Obbiars. We could not describe them because they lived in the dark, and so it was difficult to see them, but he assured me these were the Obbiar houses.

12.

The Town

THE IMMEDIATE surroundings were what we called home, but it was only a short step to the town centre and other places of interest. Although the Molineux Grounds were just around the corner, I did not take much notice of Wolverhampton Wanderers until later years, except when there was a chance of a free ticket from school to see one of the matches, usually a Reserve game. But we knew when there was a home match because our street would be full of parked cars.

Bath Road led down to the side streets which gave access to the West Park, where we could play on one of the fields, try our hand on the putting green, fish in the lake or row a boat, look at exotic plants in the beautiful conservatory, or spend a happy hour on the slides, roundabouts and swings in the children's playground. One dog we had as a pet, Sooty, a crossbred Labrador Retriever, loved the park, as he could be let off his lead to race around for a while.

Occasionally teams of Asian men would be seen playing a game similar to hockey on one of the fields, and Sooty liked nothing better than to run on to their pitch, pick up the ball and run around, being chased by the players and refusing to let go. Fortunately, they were amused by the entertaining break in their game, rather than being upset. The chalet in the middle of the Park was a refreshment room which could prove most welcome. Alternatively, just outside the Park at the Kingsland Road junction of Newhampton Road East, was what must have been one of the first local shops to sell a wide range of different flavoured ice creams out of refrigerated tubs. This was one of my father's treats when he had taken me to the Park.

Walking up Mitre Fold from home, its appearance was similar to today except that at the top on the left, where the 1980's telephone exchange extension is now, there stood a single-storey wooden building, painted green, and set in a small garden which occasionally had special displays to commemorate events, housing the Citizens' Advice Bureau. At the top of the Fold you came face to face with the large and glorious mid-19th Century Retail Market, of grey brick and stone, with its grand entrances of stone columns supporting triangular pediments, and its glazed roof giving light to the interior. To deal with the drainage of the many-pitched roof, the designer made the iron columns, which supported the roof structure, act also as down pipes. The atmosphere in here on a busy market day was something tangible. There was so much activity, so many characters, loud voices in a kind of rivalry with each other, trying to attract customers – loud enough to make a young lad feel uneasy, if he were not used to them. My favourite stall sold toys, of course, and from here was purchased for me my first (and last) violin. It was of metal, and made such a noise in the attempt to play it that I was not encouraged to keep at it.

To the north of the Market Hall was the Market Patch, where the open stalls would be brought into use on market days, and, beyond that, fronting Wulfruna Street, was another large building. This was the Wholesale Market, of red brick and yellow terracotta, erected around the turn of the 20th Century. Despite all the activity at these Markets, litter did not stay on the streets long after the Market had finished for the day.

Below here, as Wulfruna Street curved round into North Street, was the Chequer Ball Public House, followed by a row of shops, which included a Post Office and Mr Reid's establishment for gentlemen's hairdressing to the rear of a small front shop for the sale and repair of umbrellas. Mr Reid was an older person, and so his younger assistant was more popular with me, as he did not use the short-back-and-sides style which the older generation favoured. "Would you like a trim?" was his question with a smile, knowing my answer would be "Yes please."

Walking back along North Street, beyond the Market and before reaching Queen Square, you passed two shops we frequented. On the left was Hughley's cake and bread shop, and on the right was the UCP Snack Bar, which also sold food to take out. However, we avoided this after another little puppy we had, Skippy, choked to death on a chicken bone in food we had bought there. I am not sure about the blame being attached to the shop, as I

Although this photograph was taken in about 1913 there had not been much change in building by the 1950s. The grand frontage of the Queen's Arcade is prominent, with the Empire Palace on the far left. (Period Picture Postcard)

A 1920s view of Queen Square, which was not to change much by the 1950s, showing the frontage of Lyon's Café. (Period Picture Postcard)

presume we should have checked the food before giving it to him. Around the corner in Darlington Street was the chemist's we used after a visit to Doctor Jones – Gibson's – and I recollect lots of dark wood and the sort of large old-fashioned bottles of different coloured glass you could always find on high shelves in chemists at one time.

At the end of North Street where it opened out into Queen Square you would be facing the imposing façade of the Queen's Arcade, which I believe had two entrances, from the Queen Square frontage and from round the corner in Victoria Street, with the two short but elegant Edwardian arcades meeting in a circular area roofed with a glazed dome. My only recollection of a store in which I had interest here is of Stanley Gibbons stamp-collecting shop.

Also in Queen Square were a few eating establishments. At the corner of Lichfield Street above a cake shop, where the HSBC Bank is now, was the Café Royal, and two doors away the Queen's Picture House provided a restaurant facility upstairs, overlooking the Square. Where the right-hand side of the Halifax Building Society is now, Joe Lyons' cafeteria provided refreshments at everyday prices. This gave extra accommodation at a lower level at the back, with access from John Street (this part is currently called Woolpack Street), where there now stands a separate modern shop. I distinctly recall Lyons' gave me my first experience of a ring doughnut, covered in a glaze of icing, which remained a favourite. The building which until the end of March 2010 housed the Visitor Information Centre was then a select restaurant called Reynolds', again with a cake and bread shop at the front, and dining rooms upstairs. With food still in mind, the shop at the corner of Exchange Street, until recently Costa Coffee was Lipton's grocery store, and you could smell their powerful cheeses long before you reached the door.

Walking down Victoria Street you passed the front entrance and tall, smart, early Victorian façade of the Star and Garter Hotel. We certainly never went in there. Below, also on the left, was Bedford Williams, where we would go to buy linen, and shirts, socks and underpants for me. Perhaps this seemed dull, but there was a great point of interest in here. My mother would hand money over to an assistant for whatever she was buying, the assistant would write the purchase on a note, and put the note and money inside a small metal tube with a hole in one side. The tube would be placed in one of many pipes which seemed to travel all around the store, and it would disappear. Minutes later it would return to the assistant with the necessary change. Assuming the person at the other end of the pipes was honest and could count, what a safe way of dealing with things, if perhaps a little slow. How did the change always arrive back at the correct counter, I wondered. With my interest in trains, I likened it to a network of railways with stations. At the side of Bedford Williams, Farmer's Fold led past small, old, cottage style buildings with shops, to reach John Street. On the opposite side of Victoria Street was Beatties, of course, whose toy department in the basement was always popular, and where in December there would be a visit to see Father Christmas, either here or at the Co-operative Department Store in Lichfield Street, where the visit was combined with a "trip" in a vehicle, such as a space-ship or carriage, and experience a journey to reach the destination where Father Christmas was just outside. The fact that you went into this "vehicle" through one door, came out to see the man through another door, and did not have to travel back in the vehicle to be back in the store did not seem to cause children any need to question. Further down, where Barratt's of Feckenham used to be until the shop was taken over by the British Heart Foundation to sell furniture and electrical goods, was "Little Woolworth's", with a small entrance at the back from Victoria Passage leading up to the ground floor and down to the basement.

Back now to John Street, which began between the timber-framed Lindy Lou's baby and children's shop, dating from about 1500 (I do not remember it as The Copper Kettle cafe) and quite an old public house called the New Inn. The beautiful early 18th Century façade of the Old Grammar School on the right-hand side of John Street had been somewhat changed over the years. The middle section was in use as a printing works, and there were shops on each side, possibly a greengrocer's and a bookmaker's. Then the street split into two. The left hand turn would take you up towards Dudley Street, passing Manders' Paint and Varnish factory which sat on both sides. This seemed big, and I recall through one of the entrances you could see a railway track, maybe still in use for trucks to be pushed between different parts of the works.

Instead of turning left, if you carried straight on up the other arm of John Street, past another couple of shops, you would enter through an archway and up steps into what was a favourite of many local people – the Central Arcade. This was probably as old as, or maybe older than, the Queen's Arcade, but bigger and equally impressive. It was two-storeys in height, the ground floor being shops with traditional frontages, the upper floor having

Phyllis Perry and Tony, shopping in John Street, about 1957.

bay windows, always well looked after and nicely decorated, and the whole was covered by a glazed roof. Halfway up its length was a circular, domed area similar to the one in the Queen's Arcade. Just past here on the right was the Mecca for all children – Sherwood Miller's toy store. Window displays with toy soldiers and tin farmyard animals, working model railway displays, Dinky, Matchbox and Corgi toys, and a host of other sorts of attractions, made it very difficult for parents to drag children away once they were by the windows, let alone inside. For children whose parents were unable to afford to build up an electric 00 gauge model railway, Miller's could offer a cheap range of metal 000 gauge railway pieces – sections of track which slotted together, including points, steam or diesel locomotives, carriages and wagons which coupled. At the price offered, maybe one or two shillings per piece, these were obviously not even clockwork, let alone electric! But they were good fun – not made in any great detail, but quite sturdy.

You could buy some of the same toys from other shops, but Miller's was the place that stood out in people's memories. There was Meccano, and no matter how small a set you were able to afford to begin with, it could be added to, increasing the range of machines or structures you could build. A small wind-up clockwork motor would make your machine move and come alive. There was Bayco, also with different size sets, consisting of a base with tiny holes into which fitted metal rods to form the shape of a house or other building. The walls were made from plastic brick panels, red or white, with coloured doors and windows which slotted on to or in between the rods with roof units and chimneys to finish off your building. Miller's also sold toy garden sets whose name I cannot recall, consisting of a base on which you could assemble your garden with brown plastic flower beds having holes into which you could stand flowers and shrubs of your choice, lawns, pathways and trees.

At the top of the Arcade, which had an imposing Edwardian façade with shops at its corners with the street, if you turned right into Dudley Street, a former coaching inn, known as the Swan and Peacock, was a landmark. This was a three-storey timber-framed building, the upper floors jettied or overhanging, with a side access leading to the rear yard. Despite its age and architectural importance, it was demolished to make way for the C & A store, replaced by T K Max, now a Pound Shop. Also hereabouts was a specialist saddlery and leather goods shop with a fascinating window display for young eyes, including a model of part of a horse to display a saddle. It was near here

Shops on the eastern side of North Street, opposite the Molineux Hotel. These included the Post Office and Mr Reid's hairdressing shop, 1950s. (Courtesy Wolverhampton Archives and Local Studies)

where Dudley Street became Snow Hill, and where we would catch a number 35 Springhill bus (in later years nicknamed "the jive", – the old motor buses would shake and rattle) when going to visit my Grandparents at Pinfold Lane.

Turning to the left out of the Arcade you were in Dudley Street, then as now the busiest shopping street of the town centre, with "big Woolworth's", British Home Stores and Marks and Spencer's. The differences inside these stores included many more staff serving, standing behind counters with all their wares laid out, so each department or section sold its own goods, no self-selection and hunting for "please pay here" signs in those days! Outside the stores the differences included no pedestrianisation. Traffic moved slowly down the one-way street from Queen Square, there was parking at the side of the street, and narrow pavements on each side. The busyness and bustle reflected the fact that there were no such things as out of town retail parks or on-line buying – the town centre was it, but at least here you could buy anything and everything.

The section of the Ring Road which runs down from Dudley Road to Penn Road was the first part to be constructed. Before this, St John's Square presented the appearance of an almost complete Georgian Square of houses, mostly three-storeys high, some a little run-down, with the odd industrial use. Church Street, as George Street is now, was also fronted by Georgian houses. The construction of the Ring Road resulted in the loss of what could have been now, with Listed Buildings, a very smart piece of townscape.

Sometimes our walk to see Granddad Perry would be through St George's churchyard with its graves and old tombs, but pleasantly laid out and well tended. St George's Church, dating from 1830 and built in a Classical style, had an interesting interior but was grimy outside. When it became redundant, thankfully the exterior structure was saved and restored by Sainsbury's in building their new store, even if they could not save the interior. The only disagreeable aspect of the gardens was the adjoining abattoir, and on bad days the smell of burning bones was quite overpowering. Just along Cleveland Road from the abattoir stood the omnibus depot, which was later partly rebuilt and was recently used as an indoor car park. One could still see the remains of tramlines leading out into the road, despite the fact trams had not operated for twenty years or more, since they were replaced by trolleybuses.

Bilston Street began at the junction with Dudley Street, and after passing between the Savoy and Clifton cinemas it became narrower and curved towards the junction with Steelhouse Lane. There was quite a lot of old property along here, with small shops, businesses and public houses, some dating back more than 200 years. In particular I remember a couple of Queen Anne period buildings, one by the Clifton Cinema, converted to shops, the other at the corner of Walsall Street, which must have been quite a smart house in its time. These all stood in the way of progress, of course, and the wholesale demolition of the full length of one of Wolverhampton's ancient streets gave us the bleak, barren thoroughfare we have today. The Council certainly did more blitzing than Hitler.

The Queen's Building now acts as an entrance to the Bus Station. This was formerly part of a complete range of early Victorian buildings at the corner of Horseley Fields. So what we see now is only a part of what was intended by the builders for the railway company, as the entrance to the LNWR station in the middle of the 19th Century. We would turn off Horseley Fields into St James' Square to catch a bus to Willenhall or Walsall, and the service operated would alternate between the bright blue of Walsall Corporation vehicles, and the green and yellow of Wolverhampton Corporation Transport. This square also dated from the 18th Century, to judge from the architecture of its oldest buildings. Again, the Council's vision at that time was wholesale demolition of most of Horseley Fields, to create a bleak and barren area, alien to pedestrians. Of course it was not only Wolverhampton that did this – look at any large town or city and see what was lost during this period.

Father Christmas at Beatties!

On Saturdays when I was not with the cinema gang and instead was hauled off on the shopping trip, we would generally pay a visit to the Co-op grocery store in Stafford Street. I remember this as a traditional shop with goods on shelves and a counter at which you were served. Here you could leave your order for the main weekly grocery, which would be made up and delivered to your house in a cardboard box, on a specific day in the week – with us it was a Thursday. This was the first food store which I can recall being made into a small supermarket – quite a strange experience to begin with, being able to

Wolverhampton open market patch in the 1950s. The lady standing with her back to the camera in the lower left hand corner is almost certainly Phyllis Weetman to judge from her appearance, dress and stance. (Period Picture Postcard)

walk around collecting things in a basket without being stopped. Next door, on the corner of Whitmore Street, was the Co-op Butcher, who would provide the weekly meat order. We followed the butcher from here for many years when the Co-op closed and he moved elsewhere.

If the clock were turned back to the 1950s, but with present day thinking and laws on preservation of buildings and Conservation Areas of character, perhaps the Ring Road would not have been constructed so close to, sometimes actually in, the town centre. Before the Second World War there were plans to build an Outer Ring Road, some parts of which were built with wide roads. The town centre would have retained a lot more areas of character and important architecture and history.

13.

Off to the Seaside

BELL STREET was long, meandering, of a similar shape to what it was two hundred years before, when it was called Belcroft Street or Hollow Lane, probably because it followed the line of the Puddle Brook down a gradual slope before that brook was culverted. It stretched from Victoria Street all the way up to Snow Hill. Our main interest here was about half-way up on the left-hand side, where you came to Don Everall's Coach Station. This was a large area for coach parking with a small office, and a wall or solid fence at the front with the words telling you whose firm it was. From here, every June, we would set off for our two week North Wales holiday in a caravan owned by a friend of my grandmother. This was situated at Winkup's, one of those big caravan camps at Towyn, on the main road between Rhyl and Abergele. The first time we went was just after I had been in the Royal Hospital to have my tonsils and adenoids removed, at the age of six, and it was thought I needed a holiday to recuperate. The recuper-

Tony with the cuddly toy kept by Winkup's Camp, Towyn, for parents to have photographs taken of their children, about 1957.

1950s style caravan at Winkup's Camp, Towyn, near Rhyl.

ation was not helped by the discovery that I suffered from road sickness, and the coach would be forced to stop for me during the 100 mile journey, which was scheduled to have only one stop for refreshments and facilities. Once appropriate medication was found further embarrassing occurrences were stopped.

My mother and grandmother used a hairdresser named Grace Buckle, who operated a salon in her own home in Waterloo Road. She continued to do so into her seventies or eighties. Because she was a friend of the family she was known to me as Auntie Grace. I think it was her sister known as Auntie Beat who owned caravans at Winkup's, hence the arrangement by which we would rent one for the two weeks.

Winkup's Camp had its own shop and café, and shared a sandy beach, very suitable for all beach activities, with another caravan and chalet camp, next to a long, high, stone-built sea defence wall. Under this wall, on the land-side, ran a single rusty railway track, used to bring stone for maintenance. This same sea wall was the one breached by extraordinary high tides some years ago, leading to the flooding of much of the low lying countryside and the built up district of Towyn, with devastating effects on people's homes, belongings and lives. 1950s caravans did not include facilities, so there could be a walk in the early hours of the morning to the toilet block in the middle of the camp.

Climbing the walls of Beaumaris Castle, Anglesey.

The next camp to Winkup's on the main road was called Happy Days, which also had its own café, more of a restaurant, open to non-residents, where I first discovered the delights of steak and kidney pudding.

From our base we would catch the bus to Abergele and Pensarn Station, from where we would travel by train, to all sorts of interesting places in North Wales, especially those with castles, for which I had great enthusiasm. We would buy a weekly Rover ticket, which covered travel on all the lines in North Wales.

As for castles, there were Conwy, Caernarfon, Beaumaris, Cricieth, and, unlike now in later years, no rampart, turret or high ledge caused me any fear of heights. This was before the miserable Dr Beeching chopped so many railway connections between places, and when we could travel past Bangor, Caernarfon and on to Afon Wen Junction (my mother's joke was that it was so named because it was a case of "afon wen" the train comes – you could wait an hour in the refreshment room for your connection) to change for Pwllheli and Porthmadog. There was the Barmouth Radio Rail Cruise, which followed a circular route, taking in Bangor, Caernarfon, Afon Wen, Barmouth, Dolgellau, Corwen and back through Denbigh to Rhyl. It was called the Radio Cruise because there was a radio commentary piped into each carriage to give passengers information about the places we passed through.

The station staff at Abergele and Pensarn got to know us with our Rail Rover tickets and would ask each morning where we were off to explore that day. They would give advice on the train times and connections. In a side platform at the station would stand two or three older carriages converted into holiday accommodation to let. This looked an attractive proposition to me, being enthusiastic about railways, to be able to look out of the window and watch the locomotives stopping or passing through, but we never strayed from our use of a caravan.

Diesel multiple units had started to appear along the North Wales coast line by then, and the two note sound of the horn replacing a steam whistle heralded

The smallest house in Great Britain, Conwy Quay.

the approach of what was named the Green Dragon, with its red Welsh dragon emblem. Being a new idea, this was quite exciting, but of course I was unaware that within ten years all steam engines on British Railways would be replaced by diesel or electric engines. Diesels were all right, but they did not live, as did steam locomotives.

Apart from the towns with castles, we would visit Bangor, to see the Cathedral and the old pier, Menai Bridge, Llanfairpwllgwyngyllgogerych-wrndrobwllllantisiliogogogoch, where I would stand on the station platform and carefully pronounce the name, and where we would climb the Marquis of Anglesey's column to see the view, and to Holyhead to see the ferry boats to Ireland and South Stack lighthouse. Along the Conwy Valley line we would alight from the train at Betws-y-Coed and walk to the Swallow Falls. The

The Floral Hall at Rhyl promenade.

Learning road safety at Rhyl Botanical Gardens.

grown-ups did not know what the distance was from the village and how long it would take us to walk up the winding A5 to view the spectacular raging torrent, and so I would assure them every ten minutes it was "just around the next corner". At Blaenau Ffestiniog, or "blasted Ffestiniog" as my mother would call it because it always seemed to be wet whenever we went there, we would find a bus to take us to Porthmadog, to enjoy a return trip behind the double-boilered Fairlie locomotives of the Festiniog Railway, which at that time had only reached as far as a temporary terminus at Tan-y-Bwlch. Presumably this was not accessible by bus. The station at Llanrwst was just a short walk through the town and across the 17th Century stone bridge spanning the River Conwy, to the ancient mansion of Gwydir Castle with its beautiful peacocks.

The grand frontage of Gwrych Castle, Abergele.

A nearer destination than any of these was the gloriously Victorian and traditional resort of Llandudno, to see the Alice in Wonderland figures and open-air concerts in the Happy Valley on the Great Orme. We would ride on one of the tours in small, old coaches around the lower level of the Great Orme or experience the tram ride to the summit of the hill, where the building housing the café was the home of former boxer Randolph Turpin. I had heard about Dick Turpin, and so assumed the man who lived on the Great Orme must also be some sort of a highwayman.

Nearer still to our base than Llandudno was another attraction for which we had great affection. This was Gwrych Castle, romantic, rambling, its imitation defensive features combining with the comfort of an early 19th Century mansion. It nestled in the wooded hills just above, and to the west of, Abergele town, with a long drive leading up from the gatehouse on the main road through the parklands and grazing fields to the extensive range of buildings. These stretched along the side of the hill, dwindling into nothing more than a simple stone wall with occasional stone towers. Whilst I appreciated the interior of the mansion was very beautiful, my interest, apart from the fact that it was a castle, lay in the Children's Corner with its animals, and the miniature railway which had been laid next to the wall along the side of the hill. Travelling on the little train through the woods was like a journey into unexplored territory. I am saddened by the present plight of the Castle, as I am sure all who remember it will be. It has been empty, wrecked by vandals and the weather, and lies derelict, although some consolidation has taken place and a preservation trust has been set up to hopefully encourage its proper restoration and future use *www.gwrychtrust.co.uk.*

The most expensive trip we made – and it would probably still be the most expensive today – was to Llanberis, and then up to the summit of Snowdon by the mountain railway. Llanberis could still be reached by train then, being at the end of a small branch line from Caernarfon. The mountain railway was steam operated, taking an hour for the locomotive to push from behind the single coach, 5 miles up the mountain, with passing places at intermediate halts, to the platform at the top. This was just below the cairn, which was the actual summit, and the less than salubrious café which provided basic refreshments for train travellers, climbers and walkers. This café has in recent years been replaced by a much smarter building. The operation of the train was described as "weather permitting", and I recall an unexpected mist descending on one occasion once we had reached the summit, and us worrying how we were to get back down, but thankfully it was not bad enough to cancel the train. I also remember on the summit cairn my mother stepping backwards and backwards in an attempt to have us all in her box camera viewfinder. Whilst I had no fear of heights then I panicked at the thought of her disappearing over the edge and down the slope, and shouted out for her to stop – she did not seem to have been concerned.

We would sometimes catch a bus from outside Winkup's Camp for the short journey along the main road, through the district of Kinmel Bay, over the imposing Foryd Bridge which spanned the River Clwyd, past the Pleasure Beach amusement park and into the town of Rhyl itself.

A few years ago Joyce and I paid a visit to Rhyl while in North Wales, and were horrified at what had happened to the seafront – a grim, bleak, concrete bad dream had replaced the traditional promenade features fondly remembered from the 1950s. There had been pretty, well-maintained gardens and walkways, with more plant displays of variety in the Floral Hall which was like a big Conservatory. There was the traditional pier, and the expected seaside amusements. There were three theatres on the seafront – Coliseum, Gaiety and the grand Pavilion with its big, white dome that I recall hosted a circus show with animals, clowns, trapeze artistes. There had also been the Little Theatre on the edge of the town centre. Staying in a caravan, we would be looking for a mid-day meal while out and about, and in Rhyl there was another good "steak and kidney pudding" café in the town centre. The Pleasure Beach offered a variety of rides to experience, including an enjoyable if scary "ghost train", a Big Dipper and Roller Coaster (a sort of "little dipper"), plus a miniature railway which trundled around the boating lake adjacent to the River Clwyd and afforded a good view of the Foryd Bridge.

A short bus ride out of the town took us to the Botanical Gardens, where the main attraction for me was a layout of small roads, complete with small scale traffic signals, junctions, crossings, intended to help children gain road sense, by hiring one of the cycles to spend a certain time, perhaps half an hour, negotiating the roads and observing the signals – at my age it was on a large tricycle.

My father did not come with us on these holidays. He stayed at home to look after the house, maybe we could not afford for all of us to go, and also there was the question of the limited number of people the caravan could accommodate. Indeed, I think we did use two caravans owned by the same person. But Frank's sister, Auntie Phyllis, was one of the party on a few occasions, with my mother, grandmother Nora and myself. Auntie Phyllis' disability did not prevent her from being adventurous, and being the only one willing to accompany me in exploits the others shied away from, such as climbing castle towers and walking on walls.

14.

Off to the Hills

OUTSIDE Don Everall's Coach Station in Bell Street was the departure point for the "Black and White" coaches, a subsidiary of Yelloways Coaches of Cheltenham, for us to travel to Malvern, to stay with Auntie Elsie and Uncle Jim. This would be quite a long-winded journey, as we would have to pick up passengers when required at Coseley, Dudley, Brierley Hill, Stourbridge and Kidderminster. There would then be a toilet stop at Worcester, the car and coach park by the racecourse, which could be flooded if the River Severn had burst its banks. We would be set down near the shops at Malvern Link at least two hours after leaving Bell Street. I believe these coaches began their journeys at Stafford. They continued on their route from Malvern to Cheltenham, where passengers could change, after a lunch break, to other coaches of the same company which would take them on to their destinations – perhaps South Wales, Devon or even the south coast resorts. Goodness knows what time they finished their journeys!

Before the days of Dr Beeching, we were able to travel to Malvern by train to stay. The adventure would begin with a descent of steps next to the entrance to the High Level Station, along the passageway under the railway lines, with the noise and vibrations of the trains above, and out via "The Arches" to the forecourt of the Low Level Station. A bay platform here would be departure point for the local train to Stourbridge Junction, where it was necessary to change. So familiar with this journey was I, that I could reel off the names of all the stations in order between Wolverhampton and Stourbridge Junction, just in case anyone needed to know.

The "we" was usually my mother, Nan and myself. Very occasionally Frank came with us, but I do not remember my father accompanying us – he would stay at home, again to "look after the house". My Nan's closest sister was Auntie Elsie, so we would stay with her and Uncle Jim. He would meet us off the coach or train to help with carrying cases and bags and walk down to their house, a two bedroomed semi-detached council house in Duke of Edinburgh Way, which was on a small estate off the main Worcester Road at the northern edge of Malvern Link.

Uncle Jim was a big, quiet man who worked on the railways as a ganger, and before nationalisation the London Midland and Scottish Railway were his employers. Being a strong man, when he retired from the railway he found work in a removal business, whose store was housed in a former chapel on the main road in the Link, as it was and is known. As a quiet man, it was difficult to know what he was thinking. He always seemed welcoming, but with them having only two bedrooms I remember the sleeping arrangements could be difficult with my mother, Nan and myself in single beds, sharing the larger bedroom which ran from the front to the back of the house. But I also remember Uncle Jim having to sleep on a camp bed downstairs and my Nan sharing with Auntie Elsie. This seemed hard on Uncle Jim to me, although he never complained.

Their living room also ran from the front of the house to the back, but this was never used for meals. The table for eating was in the kitchen, not a big room, with a door to the back garden, one to the pantry and one to the hall. When we arrived, Auntie Elsie would have cooked lamb chops, new potatoes and runner beans grown by Uncle Jim especially for us on his allotment at the back, so we were supposed to "eat them all up". Not wanting to offend I would try, but there were occasions when I was nearly sick on stringy beans and left the remains of the dinner. The offended look was on Auntie Elsie's face, not Uncle Jim's – after all, he appreciated he could not be held responsible for the beans being stringy. Who knows if Uncle Jim used to say what he thought when we were not there? In our presence he would only go as far as staring hard at Auntie Elsie with an incredulous look, which was enough to stop her in her tracks. If she were to venture to continue saying something he did not want to hear, just a couple of firm words, "now look!" would seal her lips with a sulky expression.

Next door, Jess and George had two sons, David, and Michael who was the eldest and about the same age as myself. Michael's hobby seemed to be always finding new ways of getting into trouble, and encouraging me to join him, which I usually resisted, not seeing the fun which he did in his activities. If he knocked at the back door asking for me to come out to play, Auntie Elsie would begin by making excuses, but he did not go away, and his calling was persistent, until she would encourage me to go and play for a short while to keep him quiet. I think his mother and father appreciated my lack of wilfulness, because they would always know to scold Michael, when they found a mess somewhere, or he had dug up his father's prize plants or vegetables.

Paddle-boating on the lake in Malvern Priory Park.

Our holiday in Malvern might be for a week, or shorter – from Monday to Friday. During our stay we would go somewhere on a train or by bus on one of the days, such as Gloucester, Ledbury, Hereford, Evesham, where I might get a brief look-in at a Church or a Cathedral in between the ladies' shopping. Gloucester was their favourite, with its larger centre, and some big stores. As for the others, Auntie Elsie used to say "there is nothing much there". Once we went as far as Cirencester, the capital of the Cotswolds. After a brief look at the beautiful Parish Church and disappointment at the lack of shops, it was declared that "there was nothing much there", and it was suggested that we catch another bus to somewhere else. South Cerney was the destination chosen.

Tony with Grandmother Nora Weetman on Herefordshire Beacon, Malvern Hills.

No one knew what or where it was, but neither did they know of any of the other names on the destination board of the buses in the bus station. Whatever delights South Cerney may have for us it was where the bus turned round to go back to Cirencester with us still on it lest we should miss our connecting bus to Malvern. At least we saw the scenery through the window! We would perhaps walk up to the Link for the shops or catch a bus into town – Great Malvern. Here the Priory Church was a beautiful attraction, as was Priory Park, behind the Winter Gardens, particularly if I was let loose in one of the children's paddle boats in the lake. A walk down the hill from the town to Great Malvern Station would enable us to see Uncle Arthur at work as Station Foreman, but chatting would be cut short by a train arrival, when he was required to supervise his team and ensure passengers were dealt with properly.

But our expeditions on to the Malvern Hills were much more enjoyable. There were walks from the town, via St Ann's Well up to the summit of the Worcestershire Beacon, the highest point of the Hills, with the welcome little café which used to look out from the top. There seemed to be a good choice of Midland Red local bus services to reach different places in those days, for instance the Wyche Cutting, where the road joining Worcestershire to Herefordshire is cut through the rock, and the British Camp Hotel (now Malvern Hills Hotel), so called because of the alternative name for the adjacent hill shaped by the mounds of ancient ramparts forming rings around it at different levels. From here we would set off up the Herefordshire Beacon, to give it its proper name, and I would always have to find the Giant's Cave, just to say that I had been inside it. Noted on maps as "Clutter's Cave", it is a simple hollowed out space – it would have been a fairly small giant. On the east side of the hill we would descend to the Pink Cottage Tearoom for refreshments. The Kettle Sings, Jubilee Drive, now a more substantial establishment offering a choice of dishes, was then a very 1930s little place with its veranda at the back, nevertheless still giving inspiring views across the Herefordshire landscape towards the Black Mountains and Mid Wales on a clear day. We even went as far as walking the whole length of the Malvern Hills one day, having reached a point near to the southern end of the range by bus. This expedition we regarded as quite an achievement, if a rather tiring adventure into unknown territory, where we were warned to watch out for snakes – we never saw one.

Tony reaches the summit of Worcestershire Beacon, Malvern Hills.

The fairytale castle at Eastnor was another much enjoyed trip. We would alight from the bus to Ledbury at Eastnor Turn, then walk down to the village and the gatehouse of the spectacular Neo-Norman palace complete with battlements, lake and woodland. It still has the same breathtaking appearance fifty years later, whether viewed from the gatehouse, looking towards its grand entrance, or at the rear, across the lake enveloped by woodland to where the noble building stands high above its terraced garden.

Our few days at Malvern were never complete without visits to other members of the family. But it was always to see the sisters and brothers of my Nan and Auntie Elsie, so we would never get to meet the younger relatives, unless they happened to be there at the time. However, the older ones were kind and welcoming, with each visit being centred around the making of a pot of tea, sitting together and getting an update on who was doing what and how the children of the day did not know they were born. Occasionally, I would be brought into the conversation with a question, but most of the time I was expected to sit quietly.

There was Auntie Peggy and Auntie Nellie who had both lost their husbands. When Auntie Nellie and Uncle Frank lived in Birmingham, we would visit them by train. Auntie Nellie worked in Woolworth's, before the Bull Ring was redeveloped in the 1960s, so we might do no more than go to see her there, at her counter. They lived in the Erdington area, to the north of the City, so there was a bus ride from the City Centre, to see their new television set, as we did not have one as yet, and to watch the "Beach Ball", which was shown as a kind of test card when there were no programmes on during the day.

There was Uncle Hubert and Auntie Olive. He never seemed to be a well man, I think because of cigarettes and beer, and of their two sons and one daughter the one son, Shorty, followed in his father's footsteps. Auntie Olive was a great character, full of humour and friendship with a tireless disposition, and she was always more keen to chat to me.

Tony guards the entrance to the "Giant's Cave", Malvern Hills.

Great Malvern Station Foreman Arthur Amphlett with sisters Nora and Elsie.

There was Uncle Arthur and Auntie Floss. Arthur began at Great Malvern Station as a porter and was promoted to Station Foreman, and we would visit him there for chats, kept brief if the Stationmaster was around. To have an uncle in railway uniform made one feel important. He was not impressed by the works of Dr Beeching, and in his soft accent would complain: "He wants to do away with at least one of the three Malvern stations, look, and put people out of a job, and there'll be no stations from here to Worcester. He's going to ruin the railways in this country, look." When he had retired from the railway and we visited them at home, he always seemed to be the one who made the tea whilst Auntie Floss sat chatting. She never seemed to call him by his name – she just said "Amp", I suppose an abbreviation which had stuck. He was an interesting person to listen to, talking about his garden or his railway career, and he was more willing to chat to me than Auntie Floss. He would give us plants or cuttings to bring home. Many years later, when after Great Malvern Station had suffered a fire and was refurbished, he was invited to attend the opening ceremony, with the Head of The Western Region of British Rail being the dignitary to perform the task. This worthy person was introduced to Uncle Arthur who, when asked about his opinion, praised the work that had been done, but was not slow in telling the man what had been done incorrectly: "You've got that bit there wrong, look".

15.

Mary and Albert Fencott

C LOSER to home, after they moved to Wolverhampton, were relatives who were always friendly, kind and welcoming – Auntie Mary and Uncle Albert.

Mary Carrie-Louise Haggerty, of Leicester House, Wilton Road, Malvern, was a cousin of my grandmother Nora. She married Albert William Fencott, of Sandown Villa, Pickersleigh Road, Malvern, at Christchurch, Malvern. They both had strong local accents, perhaps his was the stronger.

Albert was an employee of W.H.Smith and Son Ltd, at their branch on Belle Vue Terrace in Great Malvern. As he transferred within the Company he moved to Witney in Oxfordshire just before they were married, then to Tewkesbury, where he became the Manager. Here they lived in a flat over the shop in the town centre, at that time occupying No 2 High Street, a three-storey Georgian property with a traditional shop front, now the premises of Dorothy Perkins, with a large old clock suspended over the pavement in the adjoining shop of the same period. On the upper floors were store rooms as well as the manager's flat, which has been empty for many years, but Dorothy Perkins' Manager advises that its rooms are still recognisable with their fitted cupboards and units. Some years later Smith's moved a couple of doors up the High Street. When I was small we visited them at Tewkesbury, by bus or coach, and their living room had its 18th Century windows looking out over the Cross, where the three main streets of the town meet.

They moved to Wolverhampton when Albert became Assistant Manager of the W.H.Smith's store, at that time in Lichfield Street, opposite the Grand Theatre. The store was frequented by permanent theatre staff or touring company personnel, and once they asked for the loan of a full set of Encyclopaedia Britannica to appear as a prop on the set of a Repertory Company production of "Semi Detached". Albert remembered that Frank had given me his 1950s set, so he suggested we might lend the books to them. In return we received complementary tickets for what was for me a first experience of live professional drama, creating a great interest in plays.

When I was quite young one of the family mentioned to Albert that I had written an imaginative children's story about three little pigs, because he worked surrounded by books, and he said he would read it and find out if it could be published. Of course I believed he was important enough to know people who produced books. Although he came back with an answer that it was perhaps not long enough to be a book, and I needed to wait until I was older, he was encouraging me not to give up, but to continue trying to write. So, thank you, Uncle Albert, for the make believe, and the encouragement.

Through some connection, possibly at the shop, Mary and Albert became tenants of a flat on the second floor of a Victorian villa in Newhampton Road East, not far from its junction with Waterloo Road. The house was owned and occupied by the firm of Fern and Partners. So we were able to see them more often. Climbing up two flights of stairs to the flat seemed to tire my family, I think because the second flight was steeper than the first. The Mr Fern in charge of the firm asked for me to go to his office on one of our visits. Although he knew who we were and would speak to us if he saw us, it seemed an odd invitation. But his intention was to pass on to me a small, thin, sharp-featured Teddy Bear which had come into his possession from somewhere. Of course we named it Ferny Bear.

Mary and Albert were strong church-goers, and would each week walk to Chapel Ash, to attend St Mark's. Later on, when they obtained the tenancy of a Council flat at the Mayfields, Willenhall Road, they changed to St Matthew's, which was quite close to their new address.

16.

Church

IT WAS not at St Peter's where I gained my first education in matters of religion, although both my Mother and Father had been pupils at St Peter's School.

I had been baptised at All Saints Church, and was taken along to Sunday School in the adjoining school buildings when old enough to take part. We have seen that my grandparents lived in the house at the left-hand end of a block of four terraced houses in Granville Street, and that in the house at the end of the accessway to the right lived very good neighbours, Violet and Edward Woodward with their daughter, Barbara, who, with her friend Eileen, taught at the Sunday School.

For a short while after we had moved to Red Lion Street, I was still taken regularly to Granville Street on a Sunday, and Barbara would call at my Grandparents to take me to All Saints. Barbara is sadly no longer with us, but Eileen has fond memories of these times.

When I changed to St Peter's I cannot say. The reason for the change was obvious in terms of easier access. My Mum continued to attend All Saints for Mothers Union Meetings or "Class", as it was called, on a weekday evening. This gave the opportunity for my Dad, as he would walk her there and back, to take my Grandfather for a drink. My Grandmother died in October 1955 when I was 4 years old, and he then remained on his own in Granville Street. Looking back, there are always things you regret, and one of mine was that I often refused the offer of my Dad to take me to visit him. The reason for refusing was probably a mixture of laziness and a preference for friends in our street, and toys or books at home. Also, at my Grandfather's everything seemed old and out of date and a musty smell lingered in each room. Who could predict that in later life I would dearly love to have met him again, and to see the contents of that house, the old furniture, fittings, pictures, clocks and ornaments, to use ourselves, or perhaps offer to a museum keen to make good use of some of these in their displays? However, in my early years, in a corner of my Grandfather's living room was still kept that same box of toys for me to play with.

So the visits to Granville Street became infrequent, as I changed to St Peter's. I suppose because I started at St Peter's at such a young age and spent the growing years there, everything about it was considered normal and taken for granted. Maybe I thought that, to be really special, a place of worship had to be a Cathedral or an Abbey. It was not until many years later that I returned with Joyce to a main Sunday service at St Peter's, and I received a feeling of being completely overcome with – something almost tangible. Yes, it is special – it is Grade I listed, has lots to do with local and national history, outstanding architectural features, has upheld a great tradition of music with its choirs – but it is more than this. Perhaps it is because the Church is so drenched in the power of over one thousand years of worship and prayer, that it can do much to help one keep hold of a faith that took many years to return or be re-activated.

Where the University's St Peter's Square modern building entrance stands now, there was a large late Victorian building, St Peter's Institute, in the old St Peter's Square, which was then a side street off Wulfruna Street, behind the Wholesale Market. The ground floor was of ordinary height, and contained various rooms. This was where Sunday School was held each week for the youngest children. We learned the Catechism, sang hymns and collected picture stamps in small booklets, to show how regular our attendance was, and to learn about the Bible stories depicted on the stamps. Upstairs was a large hall, with a steeply pitched roof and a high oriel window at the front overlooking the street. In this hall the older children would meet for worship, and then split into four different groups for lessons, each group being led by its own teacher. I remember Miss Roper and Margaret Stallard were two of these well-liked teachers. Members of the clergy would join us sometimes for the worship and to see how we progressed. I recall Father Able, Father Grace, and a young Deacon, Mr Brown, later ordained, who were all as popular as the teachers. So the total complement for the Sunday School was quite high.

The annual Sunday School outing would usually be undertaken in an old boneshaker of a double-decker bus, which would take an age to get anywhere. As I was prone to road sickness, the bus would not need to travel many miles before having to pull in at the side of the road for a little green-faced lad to jump off just in time. This was before the discovery of travel sickness tablets. The Sunday School outing would generally be to some recreational park such as Alton Towers, Trentham Gardens or Drayton Manor Park. These were rather tame in those days, in that they lacked the modern horrific rides, but we enjoyed them nevertheless.

Confirmation classes led to the confirmation service in St Peter's on Palm Sunday by the Bishop of Lichfield, to enable First Communion to be taken on Easter Sunday, which made it feel special. Before then, and to observe what the ministers did at a communion service, I would obtain a grandstand view from the Gallery at the west end of the Church. This dates back to 1610, has some lovely carving in the wood, and was paid for by the Merchant Taylors' Company, to be used by the boys of the Wolverhampton Grammar School. To be able to join the rest of the congregation in receiving communion made one feel quite grown-up. Canon John Brierley was the Rector then, a man of great presence – a young lad would stand in awe of him.

The enforced move away from Red Lion Street and the town centre in 1962 made travel to the services and Sunday School, or Bible Class as it became known for older children, more difficult. Also, we were told to observe a strict rule, not to eat anything less than three hours before communion. I look back at my Father valiantly trying to cook Sunday breakfast in time for me to eat it, and my becoming cross when it was apparently too late for me to go to the service. This was the result of a bad rule I felt I should observe. In time my attendance at Church came to an end, and although a faith remained in a small way, it was not to be rekindled for many years.

17.

Entertainment

THE CINEMA was popular with local people in the 1950s, before television ownership became so widespread. A group of us children from Red Lion Street would set off each Saturday morning to the 10am Matinee programme at the Odeon in Skinner Street, later converted to a three-screen cinema, then a Bingo Hall, now a Banqueting Suite, only a short walk for us via Townwell Fold.

The inside of the Odeon was quite grand. I learned in later years that this was because it was a Harry Weedon design of 1937 for the owner of the Odeon chain, Oscar Deutsch, with his special style, the subdued lighting hidden behind the layered arches stepping back from the main proscenium arch, and it was considered an important Odeon because Mr Deutsch himself attended the opening.

The admission price for us children at these morning shows was 6d in the Stalls and 9d in the Circle. With my pocket money of half a crown, to go in the Stalls would leave me with two shillings to spend, either on sweets inside, or in the shops afterwards. The programme usually lasted for two hours, and would contain a cartoon, a cliff-hanging episode of a serial such as Zorro or some similar super-hero, and a feature film. Generally we were well behaved compared with some of the audience, but nevertheless we did err one Saturday, when we were ejected by the staff for fighting, and told not to return.

We switched loyalty to the Savoy, in Bilston Street, which was to be re-named the ABC and then latterly the Cannon, for a while, until we were removed from that establishment also, for swearing at the usherettes. The

Savoy was of a similar age to the Odeon, but with less decorative features, inside and outside, but still the 1930s Art Deco style. A hesitant return to the Odeon proved successful – our faces were not remembered by the attendants. Probably only the faces of those regularly removed for misbehaving were familiar enough for them to recognise.

Small plastic model kits of aeroplanes and ships, by Airfix and other makers, could be purchased for two shillings each. Larger ones cost a little more. A tube of plastic cement would be 6d. Often the return home from the cinema would take a detour through Beatties' toy department, or there would be a visit to one of the other stores with a toy counter selling the models, such as British Home Stores, where the remainder of the week's pocket money would be spent on one of these kits. Saturday afternoon would then be taken up with gluing together and painting and adding the transfers to the latest acquisition, by Geoff and myself.

There were other cinemas in the town centre. We would sometimes go to the Odeon or Savoy to see the main film programme of the week, if of interest to youngsters, or to the Gaumont, Snow Hill, or the Clifton, opposite the Savoy. This would perhaps be on the Saturday afternoon, with a plea for extra pocket money.

On the site of the Gaumont now stands Wilkinson's Store. The Gaumont was from memory larger in size than the others, and with another distinct style of the 1930s. It had a stage large enough to host live variety shows, and my mother took me to see one such show with star pianist Russ Conway topping the bill. In the 1960s the Beatles appeared there. I missed that but did see the Rolling Stones in 1965 – I only say "saw" because it was impossible to hear most of their songs, the low amplification in those years being insufficient to raise the sound level above the deafening screams of the girls in the audience.

The Clifton was demolished to widen Bilston Street, where the Police Station now fronts the street. Whilst the others were purpose-built cinemas with a single circle, and dating from the 1930's, the Clifton had previously been a live theatre, with Stalls, a Grand or Dress Circle, and an Upper Circle or Balcony, which was only used when the cinema was packed for a popular film. There were also Boxes, one on each side, and all were decorated in an ornate Victorian style, with origins in the 1860's, although there had been some reconstruction after a fire. The screen was at the back of the stage, but because of the rake on the stage floor it was still possible to see films when

The decorative façade of the Prince of Wales Theatre, Bilston Street, built 1863.
(Courtesy Wolverhampton Archives and Local Studies)

After undergoing a few changes from being the Prince of Wales, the Clifton Cinema before being converted into a Bingo Hall in 1966. The decorative façade of the upper floors remained unchanged, apart from the parapet hiding the projection room. (Courtesy Wolverhampton Archives and Local Studies)

sitting near the front of the Stalls. Some rows of seats in the Stalls were not securely fixed to the floor – a source of amusement to us children, in seeing how far they could be rocked. The whole interior had a musty smell about it. Nevertheless we enjoyed our films there as much as in the more modern establishments, perhaps because, having been a live theatre, and with its different architecture, it had quite a different and special atmosphere. Amongst visits there I recall my father taking me to see the epic "Ben-Hur" with Charlton Heston. It was so popular we had to sit towards the back of the Balcony – "The Gods" as it was nicknamed.

Apart from these cinemas I believe I was taken to the Scala in Worcester Street which closed in 1956 to become a Bingo Hall, and the Queen's in Queen Square, which ceased showing films to become a dance hall in 1959. Both of these are long since gone.

Out of town the Penn Cinema at Warstones Road was a favourite, being close to my grandparents' house. Being on the second circuit it received the main feature films later than in town, but some people would wait to see the pictures they wanted and go to the "Penn". They felt it was a friendly and comfortable place. Perhaps not so grand as the big town centre establishments, it still had a lovely 1930s style and was always very well looked after and remained a favourite of mine until it closed in 1973. A supermarket now occupies the site.

The winter Pantomime at the Grand always provided at least one visit per year to the live theatre. Occasionally there would be a second, to see something equally of interest to children, such as an Easter special of Peter Pan, with Julia Lockwood in the title role, flying above the stage on wires, and her mother Margaret Lockwood playing Mrs Darling. An alternative might be a variety show such as those starring comedy duo Jewell and Warriss, or an up-and-coming pop singer called Adam Faith, complete with screaming girls in the audience.

I was not five years old when the Hippodrome in Queen Square burnt down, but I can recall the horror of looking through the gaping doorways in the back wall of the stage in Cheapside, to see the charred and smouldering rubble, and pieces of the two circles hanging precariously, whilst the beautifully ornate front facade in the Square remained intact. It was thought the fire had been started by a cigarette on the carpet which someone had failed to put out. It was such a cold February night that this happened, that the water was freezing as it came out of the firemen's hoses. I was taken to this Theatre

The ornate front of the Empire Palace Theatre, Queen Square, built in 1898 on the site of a smaller Music Hall, at the time of its opening. (Courtesy Wolverhampton Archives and Local Studies)

The spectacular interior of the Empire Palace, showing Stalls, Grand Circle and Upper Circle, with side boxes, and elaborate ceiling. (Courtesy Wolverhampton Archives and Local Studies)

once, probably not long before the fire, to see their winter Pantomime, but can remember little other than the impression of a wicked witch standing at the front of the stage. I suppose I was too young to appreciate the wonderful interior. It had been built in 1898 as the Empire Palace, replacing an earlier, smaller, Victorian Music Hall. After some alterations in 1922 it changed its name to the Hippodrome. Sadly it was not rebuilt after the fire. The bleak looking store, built to replace the Hippodrome, was occupied by Times Furnishing, and then Poundstretcher, before Yates' Wine Lodge brought some semblance of design back to the Queen Square façade.

18.

School

UNTIL the building of an Asda Superstore just to the north of Wolverhampton Wanderers' Molineux football ground, there stood on roughly the same site Red Cross Street School, which we have seen was well known to my parents when they were children and where I took the first hesitant steps across the playground of the Infants' section at the age of four and three quarters. Some children were known to have been upset at the wrench from their parents into the hands of a strange new guardian in this strange new environment. Parental worries that I too would be a reluctant pupil were soon swept away. Mrs Richards, my first teacher, an older lady as I recall, was a welcoming person, to whom I took an instant like and my willingness to go into school, compared with other children at other schools, was attributed to her character. When my mother apprehensively walked with me towards her, I took Mrs Richards' hand without any sign of worry and accompanied her into the school quite happily. Other infants' schoolteachers with whom I spent time were a young Mrs Griffiths and an older Mrs Dent. The former I remember with a sense of dislike, on account of her sharpness, but the latter, I am told, had no trouble in encouraging me to work, and was a kind person.

The School had a frontage to Red Cross Street, but also had entrances to both the Infants' and the Junior sections from the next one parallel to it, Birchfield Street. The classrooms of the Infants' school faced south on to the playground, the high classroom windows being partly protected by the veranda running the length of the block.

The Art Deco designed Assembly Hall was also used for various activities, in addition to the short assembly service which started the day.

There was "Music and Movement", a kind of fitness class with the aid of the radio or music, and the occasional special treat of a play or pantomime was supplied by visiting groups of players. One such performance was "Hansel and Gretel", when the stage was formed by simple curtains, with a central scene, behind which the players changed and prepared for their entrances and exits.

I remember a lesson where children were being asked by Mrs Griffiths what work their fathers did. Most of the houses in Red Lion Street being occupied by members of the Police Force or Fire Service, she asked if my father was a Policeman. I said no. Was he a Fireman? I said no again. Well what was he, she asked, somewhat impatiently. Of course, I had little knowledge of the office job in a factory which Dad did, and so I blankly replied: "He's just a man." This met with some laughter from within the class, but with derision by the teacher – Mrs Griffiths encouraged the other children to laugh, and heightened my embarrassment with her comments. The only way I could remove myself from this very uncomfortable position was to ask if I could go to the toilet, and thankfully she agreed. A reluctant return to the class, expecting some kind of punishment, was followed by a long period of apprehension at going to school, I suppose because of her treatment, this incident being probably the worst one. I was the one to be picked upon, as I do not recall any of the others being treated in the same way.

In the Junior School my first teacher, Mrs Darby, was a pleasant and kind person. Her son John became a school friend through to the age of eleven, and we would visit each other's houses. At a young age he had already formed a desire to enter the profession of dentistry, something that was beyond my comprehension, wandering around inside people's mouths, and a visit to the school dentist not being top of my list of favourite things to do. They lived in a smart Edwardian house overlooking West Park, where Mrs Darby also taught music. Mrs Darby's class was followed by Miss Gregory's and then Miss Brookshaw's for the two years leading up to the "Eleven Plus" examination. Miss Gregory was perhaps middle-aged, had red hair and a fiery temper to match. In her moods she would throw things at anyone who annoyed her – pencils, rulers, books, blackboard rubber, anything that came to hand, would come flying through the air towards their target, much to our alarm, as her aim was not always accurate. Thankfully I was never aimed at for anything I did, either from the missiles or the smack across the back of the hand with the ruler which was another of her sharp reminders.

Teacher looking bemused at her class of twins in Red Cross Street Infants' School in 1955. (Photograph used with permission of Wolverhampton Express and Star)

The Headmaster when I began was Mr David, a kindly and helpful gentleman, who was very fond of the school, and became a little emotional on giving his farewell speech at his retirement, so much so he had to suddenly grip the side of the table he was standing next to. He was replaced by the Infants' School Head, Mrs Llewellyn-Davies.

I think my own mother and Sally's mother from Red Lion Street used to take Sally and myself to school or meet us afterwards, with the occasional treat of sweets from the nearby shop, at the bottom of Birchfield Street, before our return home up Molineux Street, until we were old enough to walk on our own. I was about eight years old when I lost the person by whose means I first found what was attractive about girls, when Sally and family moved away.

From then on I would walk to school on my own. It was a ten minute walk, which was in those days thought to be perfectly safe for a child. However, I did find more companions. At the corner of North Street and Molineux Street was the cobbler's shop and house of Mr & Mrs O'Connor and their two daughters Susan, who was a year older than myself, and Pamela, a little younger. So occasionally I would walk down with one or both of these. The interior of Mr O'Connor's shop was saved and preserved as the interior of

A later picture of what had been Miss Gregory's class in Red Cross Street Junior School. (Photograph taken by, and used with permission of, Mr David Watson)

the cobbler's premises at the Black Country Living Museum. A couple of doors further on from their property lived a very quiet lad, younger than me, called Peter, whose mother waited with him at the front door for me to pass by, and began asking if I would walk with him down to the school. Perhaps they had only just moved into the area and she was worried about him.

It was on Wednesday lunchtimes, when my Step Grandfather Frank had to come into town to bring his books to the office of the "National", that he used to meet me from school and come back to Red Lion Street for dinner. On our way we would call in at a little newsagents' shop at the lower end of North Street, run by Mr Piggott, for chocolate or sweets. Here I was told not to ask questions about the small boxes on display with revealing pictures of women on the cover and films inside. Here also I discovered an interesting children's weekly magazine called "Knowledge" with lots of facts and information. I think Frank expected that I would want him to buy it for me for a couple of weeks, but I explained it ran for a whole year to make up a set. "How long?" he said incredulously. But he was happy to carry on, and so eventually I built up a little encyclopaedia.

Miss Brookshaw was an exceptional teacher, to whom I owed a lot, a middle-aged, stocky person with grey hair and thick glasses. She could be hard on lazy or downright naughty children. I remember Robert, the local bully, being caught treading and standing on other children's feet. Miss Brookshaw, quite a big lady, did for him what he had done for others, saying "Let's see how you like it, Robert," before standing him in the corner. He winced and his eyes watered but he did not shout out. I think he was a little quieter for a while after this episode.

But to those willing to work and learn she devoted much time and patience in helping them improve. She kept a "library" of books in a bookcase outside the classroom in the corridor, from which we were encouraged to borrow books to read. However, the rule was only one Enid Blyton at a time. She also believed in organising Parent/Teacher events and meetings, where she could chat to mothers and fathers about the progress of the children and make suggestions as to how to help. Some of us had skipped a year in the Juniors, which meant that we joined Miss Brookshaw's class with a number of children who were a year older, but we stayed in her class for a second year. During this period, and partly as a result of the enthusiasm of Miss Brookshaw, I discovered an interest in drama. I suppose the theatre visits had started this off, but once a week we had a drama class, when we would use the stage of the Juniors' Assembly Hall to act out plays and charades we made up ourselves. A small group from the class might think up a word of more than one syllable, act out a small scene for each syllable, then a final one for the whole word. The rest of the class were then invited to guess the word. I looked forward eagerly each week to these classes, and maybe thought I would grow up to be an actor. One of the girls in the class who was keen, and very good, at drama, was Helen, who became an accomplished professional actress, Helen Roberts. In Red Lion Street some members of the gang were also interested in acting to varying degrees, and this would encourage us to make up imaginary situations and stories.

One teacher whose junior school class I was never part of, except for craft work, which including making things in wood and cardboard, was Mr Gardiner, a generally quiet but mean teacher who was known for the punishment of children in his own class. We used to go the Central Baths near West Park once a week for a swimming lesson of about an hour, with one of the teachers to supervise. One week Mr Gardiner was in charge of the party and for some reason we were late getting back for our school dinner. Several of the class at the front of the group ran across North Street, when we reached the top of Red Cross Street, to hurry towards the school dining rooms in Red Hill Street. His cool, calculated way of dealing with the particular children who should have stopped and waited for the teacher to guide them across the road was to give all of us, whether we had crossed the road or not, a good hiding on the backside with a plimsoll in the afternoon. His class was always taught by a man, Mr Gardiner replacing Mr Cordey, and being in his turn replaced by Mr Hunt, who came from Whitmore School, where, the rumour was they used electric caning machines.

The right-hand side of Red Hill Street leading up the slope from North Street was the site of the school kitchens and dining rooms. I persevered with the daily dinners there for a while, but I think Mum and Dad received the message that I was not happy with the food they presented, which included eating a raw carrot after the meal, which made me sick, and I was back to going home for dinner. After all, it was not all that far to walk, Mum's cooking was better, and perhaps it helped not to have to pay for the school dinners.

Red Hill Street was also the site of the home of the girl who was my second "crush" in these early years – Janet Monnes. I went to one birthday party at her house, which was the first on the right as you walked up the street, in a terrace of small cottages.

I can recall some of the names of children in the class. There were two Roberts, Williams and Jenks, two Johns – Darby and Carter, Colin Wilbrey, a Richard, and a Michael Jenks. Also there were other pretty girls in the class – Catherine Powis, Barbara Handley, Christine Maiden, Sandra White, Susan Jenks (Michael's twin, I believe), another Barbara – Rhodes – and an Ann Ashford, but obviously Janet had something special. We sat at double desks, and in Miss Brookshaw's class of about forty children, John Darby sat next to me on the left-hand side of the room, so that he could crib off me when necessary, although he would hide his own work when I got stuck, or give me the wrong answer. For instance, I did not have a clue who invented television – this was one of the questions we were asked in a test – and he quite seriously told me it was John Yogi Bear. Of the girls mentioned, Ann and one of the Barbaras sat to the right of us, Susan and Sandra in the middle of the room, and the other four girls were behind us. Janet was immediately behind us, but if I tried to take advantage of this closeness to express appreciation of her I would be pushed away. Next to her was Christine Maiden, then behind them were Catherine Powis and Barbara Handley.

I suppose it was during this period that I should have realised I possessed no attributes which girls found attractive. One girl, Lesley, who was also quite pretty and from a well-off family living in quite a smart house near West Park, invited a number of children from school including myself, to her birthday party one year. I found I was one of those ignored by her and her inner circle at this party. Nevertheless the following year, when Miss Brookshaw asked for a show of hands of those who were going to Lesley's forthcoming birthday party, I put up my hand expectantly along with several others. Lesley piped up: "Oh, Tony's not invited to the party, Miss." I think I went bright red and wished I could disappear somewhere. She went on to marry a Wolves Footballer.

Miss Brookshaw arranged for several members of the class to have penfriends at the school in the Shropshire village of Ditton Priors. We were encouraged to write to each other, and a coach trip to see them was organised. My penfriend was Robert Whitefoot, whose family ran a farm there, and we, together with some of the others, were taken

The end part of the hall of Red Cross Street Juniors' School. (Photograph taken by, and used with permission of, Mr David Watson)

on a walk up the slopes of Brown Clee, the highest hill in Shropshire. My friendship faded, it was suggested by family because Robert bought me a penknife as a present, and I failed to give him a coin in response to save the friendship being cut.

Children can be extremely cruel to each other. I passed the "Eleven Plus" examination, with a sufficiently good mark to achieve a place at the Wolverhampton Grammar School, at that time, of course, not independent, but it did retain a small degree of independence from other Local Authority schools. This was achieved by a Consolidated Fund to help towards the purchase of books and materials. Each boy's parents would contribute 30 shillings per term to this fund. My Mum and Dad struggled to buy the school uniform, satchel, P.E. and games kit which were obligatory for all pupils. What was looked upon by parents and teachers, especially Miss Brookshaw, as something to be proud of, was viewed with distaste by certain others within the class. No one else in my year was going there, although Malcolm Bayliss, who went on to become a solicitor in his father's firm, from the year before me, had already won a place there from Red Cross Street, and a couple of the girls were going to the High School for Girls. So I was given the title of a "snob". How could I be a snob, I wondered. We did not live in a large house, have lots of money, or speak with posh voices. But snob I was dubbed.

So Red Cross Street Primary held some good memories, and some others which have obviously lain beneath the surface all these years and were not so good.

I am very grateful to Friends Reunited for enabling me to contact people who in these days were amongst the children I knew. From the contacts made, the following have written their own reminiscences and have given permission for these to be included, for which I thank them, and also I thank Christine Wright, née Maiden, for use of her photographs taken at the time of the Ditton Priors trip.

Red Cross Street Schools – Catherine Powis, now Simpson

My recollections of the school are mainly as Tony has recorded them – although he will be pleased to know that I have no recollection of his two embarrassing moments! I've added here a few other items that may be of interest. As I have been thinking about this I find that I gradually recall more and more.

In addition to the infants and junior schools there was also a nursery class. I went to this for one term prior to starting in the infants. Unlike the remainder of my time at Red Cross Street, I did not like the nursery class at all. There were two reasons for this: it was compulsory to stay for lunch, and after lunch there was an afternoon sleep. Little camp beds were brought out and we were all expected to sleep for the given period (no idea how long). By the age of 4 most children have given up afternoon naps and consequently I used to lie awake for the entire period. If when the sleep period ended any children were still asleep they would be left where they were until they woke up while afternoon nursery resumed around them.

(Left) Red Cross Street Junior School Teacher Miss Brookshaw with one of her flock during the school visit to Ditton Priors. (Right) Christine Maiden to the right of her penfriend during the Ditton Priors visit. (Photographs by and with permission of Christine Wright)

At the start of every new school year, maybe at the start of each term even, there would always be children crying and clinging to their mothers, obviously afraid of being left. I am happy to say that I never felt like that, I was always certain that my mother would return for me. Thirty years later when my own children started school I witnessed the same scenes once more, but fortunately not from my children.

The Infants' School building was as Tony described it. I remember Mrs Dent as being the teacher of the oldest class but I do not remember the other two teachers Tony mentioned. I thought that the teacher of the first class was a Miss MacDonald who I remember as a very kind, elderly (probably middle-aged) woman with a bun.

However, the one memorable event that happened in the Infants (I have checked this with my mother who is sure it occurred while we were in the Infants) was the arrival in the school of the two little Indian girls – Tasina and Amia (no idea if these are the correct spelling). They were the first coloured children that I, and probably most of the other children, had ever met. To the girls, they were fascinating – so pretty with long thick black hair and different clothes. Maybe they did not appear so fascinating to the boys! They could not speak English when they first arrived so although there was a 2-3 year age difference they were put in the same class, which was very thoughtful of the Head. I cannot remember whether this was our class or not. I think that Tasina was about our age with Amia being younger. Although other coloured and black children must have come to the school in the years that followed, the only two that I can remember are Tasina and Amia.

In the Juniors I remember Mrs Darby, Miss Gregory (very strict but excellent teacher) and Miss Brookshaw. I do not remember anyone who taught the 2nd class (the one we missed) although I had a feeling that there was at least one change of teacher for that class. The Head was a Mr David when we started but I think he retired and the Infant Headmistress became Head of both Infants and Juniors.

Each morning there would be assembly in the Hall. The teachers obviously liked singing and sometimes the classes performed for each other. The singing teacher(s) seemed to particularly like singing in 'rounds'. I assume that when the classes all performed it took place as an extension

Believed to be Catherine Powis and Barbara Handley walking up Brown Clee Hill during school visit to Ditton Priors. (Photograph by, and with permission of, Christine Wright)

of the morning assembly but I may be wrong. After assembly the first lesson each day was always arithmetic. I think this lasted until the morning break. There must have been a proper timetable but other than always having arithmetic I do not know what it was. We learned our tables but *not* by chanting out aloud.

The Junior school playground was in two parts, three if you count the small area by the Red Cross St entrance. In one part of the playground, the part that faced North St, the boys always played football. Boys who did not want to play football and the girls played in the main part that was bordered by the classrooms. I remember playing with skipping ropes and hide and seek type games. There were also the little bottles of milk for morning break.

I lived in Dunstall Avenue, which meant I walked to school along Waterloo Rd and up Red Cross Street. I usually walked with Barbara Handley who lived in the same road. There were a lot of children from the school who lived in the neighbouring streets. Half way up Red Cross Street on the left hand side was a side road and on the corner was a little sweet shop. It was the traditional type of sweet shop with the penny sweets in jars, red liquorice laces, flying saucers etc. You could buy a packet of chewing gum which contained a card of a film star, the idea being to collect the set. There were supposedly 40 cards in the set but I suspect only 37 were produced! All of the children who passed went in there – I wonder now if the shop ever had any adult customers. A little old lady kept it – she seemed to perfectly match the shop.

As we got older Barbara and I sometimes varied our route to school. We could take a short cut that brought us out in the street with the sweet shop on the corner, thereby cutting off the corner of Waterloo Road and Red Cross Street. One advantage of this route was that we passed a paper making works that sold off bundles of scrap paper for a few pence.

I remember all of the girls Tony mentioned with the exception of Susan who I cannot recall at all. Also, there was another Barbara, three in total, although one of them left the class for a while and then returned. I think she had TB and had been in a sanatorium (I may be wrong, but she was away because of a spell in hospital). Also there was Elaine, she sat by Ann. I cannot remember so many of the boys; there was Tony and John, two Davids, two Roberts, one of whom was the year above. There were two boys Billy and Colin who lived near me but I am not sure if they were the year above. By the time we were in Miss Brookshaw's class we had integrated quite well with the children who were a year older and were quite friendly with some of them. I remember Jennifer, Helen, Geoffrey, Malcolm and the twins Brenda and Brian.

I think there must have been quite a few children who started or left the school over the time we were there. In the infants there was a girl in our class from a desperately poor family, who also lived quite near me. At one stage the Health Visitor/Social Services (?) shaved her head presumably to get rid of lice. I remember feeling so sorry for her. Yet I cannot remember her being there by the end of the Juniors. In Mrs Brookshaw's class a boy arrived who was not able to play outside at break time because he had brittle bones. I remember him entertaining us with tales of all of the broken bones he had suffered.

When we were in Miss Brookshaw's we had pen friends in a small village near Bridgnorth called Ditton Priors and we visited there as our school trip. The children were mainly from farming communities. I think they also visited

Red Cross St. Another school trip I remember was a visit to the fire station – we walked there.

When we were in Miss Brookshaw's class there was a library (well, a cupboard in the corridor outside the classroom) that we were encouraged to borrow from. The rule was something like only one Enid Blyton at a time. If we wanted to borrow more than one book at a time the other book had to be by a different author. Nevertheless I managed to gradually work my way through all of the Enid Blyton's in that cupboard.

Despite the fact that a large number of the children in the class were far from being academic, so were probably not that interested in the lessons, I do not remember any bad behaviour in any of the classes.

Then, we sat the 11 Plus and went our separate ways. Janet and myself went to the Girls High School. I too remember being called a snob.

Catherine Simpson (née Powis)

School Memories – Barbara Handley

I grew up in an Edwardian terraced house in Dunstall Avenue, Wolverhampton, Staffordshire. It had a small front garden which was unusual in that area then. The houses in most of the streets opened directly onto the pavements. Mr Norman Bishton owned a lot of houses including ours. At that time it was a small cul-de-sac with three grand houses at the far end. At the open end stood a small house, originally the lodge for the large houses which we called "The Privates!" Mrs Lane lived there with her sons Walter and Donald. Sometimes we would press our faces against the gates to the houses and watch the maids, in their black and whites, walking the dogs. I can only remember poodles. I think one house was Morley House and another Dunstall House. I remember the Recorder lived in one and a Mr Meynells. Eventually Morley House became a YMCA hostel and I remember the Mayor visiting it. Mrs Winston Churchill opened it on July 6th 1950.

Back to my house. My father and his parents were the first family to live there. They moved in about 1908/09. My father had been born in West Street in July 1907. At that time the house number was 12 but on building houses opposite it became no 23. Catherine Powis lived at the newer no 12.

Further along the avenue were some allotments and I was always thrilled to be taken to see the pigs there. The allotments were locked and so it was a privilege when my Uncle Tom Egerton took me in. He was married to my father's cousin Nellie and they lived next door with her sister Edith Cadman. We children were very lucky to grow up in a quiet cul-de-sac as we could play safely out in the road.

Around our front garden we had a low wall and a privet hedge. On the walls were the marks from when the railings were removed for the war effort. As the name suggests I lived in a road with trees planted all along our side. There were lime trees which covered everything with their sticky resin.

My first school was Red Cross Street Primary School. Although it was an inner city school deprived in many ways e.g. we had no playing field, the teachers were really good and had good results. In my year, I passed the 11 plus to go the Municipal Grammar along with John Darby, Christine Maiden and Sandra White. Tony Perry went to the Boys' Grammar and Catherine Powis to the Girls' High.

In the Infants I remember the paddling pool outside Mrs Richard's classroom. I also remember the daily nap in the hall for the young ones. I think I was in Mrs Richard's class first. At the time I thought she was quite elderly. It would be interesting to know how old she actually was! Then it was Mrs Griffiths who I cannot really remember. Following her was Mrs Dent. I remember liking Mrs Richards and Mrs Dent.

In the Junior School I was in Mrs Darby's class at the same time as her son. They lived in Park Road East near the West Park. I remember skipping a year, but do not know which teacher I missed. I was now in Miss Gregory's class. I do not remember actually getting into any trouble with her myself but she was a scary person. I remember many airborne missiles but in particular the board duster! At this time I was mostly with older children and enjoyed helping the slower ones with their reading, which I was to do again later in life. Miss Brookshaw in charge of the top class was an excellent dedicated teacher. My mother was a member of the P.T.A. and she said Miss Brookshaw often brought some pupil's knitting to meetings and put it right there. She never stopped. If you were keen she would always support you. I was a little afraid of her in a respectful way. She was no doubt one of the best teachers of her day. As I had skipped a year I spent two years in her class. I think she lived in nearby Dunkley Street. On the whole I was very happy at Red Cross Street School.

I remember when the first immigrants started to appear in Waterloo Road. Eventually we had a few at our school. One name has stuck with me. Pansy Gordon. The West Indian girls had such exotic names. I also befriended an Asian girl who spoke no English. It was eventually discovered that she was of

The Art Deco assembly hall of Red Cross Street Infants' School. (Photograph taken by, and used with permission of, Mr David Watson)

an age for Secondary school and was transferred to Whitmore. At the bottom of Red Cross St lived the Kumars. Sorry I do not know which number! One Christmas we had a draw to take home the school Christmas tree, and a Sikh boy won it. I hope his parents enjoyed the surprise.

A slum clearance began in the area and there were many derelict buildings around. We used to go exploring the houses and shops in North Road which only had a few floorboards to balance on. I do not know what my parents would have thought of my adventures! These properties were eventually replaced by high rise flats.

My main friends from this school were Catherine Powis, David and Susan Harriman, Helen Roberts (the actress), Jennifer Martin, Sally Edes, whose father was a policeman and lived in Red Lion Street, Lesley Wernick and Christine Maiden. Christine used to feed my cats when we were away. I remember going to Lesley's house in Park Avenue and seeing her Wendy house. Of course she belonged to Wernicks, the shed builders and the house was very special. Sally left to go to another school but I was reunited with her at the "Muni". Geoffrey Glazzard became a top showjumper. I remember the O'Connor sisters who I was friendly with. I think their cobbler's shop is now in the Black Country Living Museum. Nearby Billy Turley lived at the Fox Inn next to Molineux. I also remember Susie Parker, Ann Ashford, Robert Williams, the Jenks twins, Geoffrey Stanworth, Peter and Robert Durnall, Colin Wilbury, David Hood, Barbara Rhodes, the Baggott twins, Carol Goodwin, Billy Ridgeway, Pamela Gibbons, whose father had a TV or electrical shop, and Robert and Gerald Bramhill. Older pupils were Roger Guy, Gill and Janet Watkins who all lived in Dunstall Avenue.

Helen Roberts starred in two television series of "Now We are Seven". She has also appeared in advertisements for the Welsh Tourist Board and Welsh language programmes. She actually moved to Wolverhampton from Wales on the death of her mother and lived with her father's sister in Dunstall Road. Sadly she has suffered from ill health in recent years.

I remember my elderly Welsh doctor, Doctor Jones on Waterloo Road. Across the road was my dentist, Mr Melville Darby, a relative of classmate John Darby. At one time I have discovered my paternal grandmother was in service in Waterloo Road, working for a dentist. The houses were very grand and occupied by professional people. Nearby was Wadhams Hill and I remember taking a limping pigeon to the P.D.S.A. there!

Closer to home was Dunstall Hill. Occasionally we children would venture to the top, to what were known as the garden hills. It was another world up there. There were lanes of allotments hidden by high hedges. We always felt we were in forbidden territory and were very daring to go there. Also at the top of the hill, we could look down over the steam engines workshop on Stafford Road. This was a railway workers area and many men had moved to Wolverhampton to work there. Small houses were built to house them. Off Dunstall Hill was West Street, where my father was born, Ewins St and Dunstall Street. Later demolished and replaced by Do-It-All. Children from those streets thought we were posh because we had front gardens.

Next door to me in Dunstall Avenue were Mary and Ken Wilmot, their two sons John and David, and Mary's aunt Annie Cuss. They ran the Methodist Chapel Bethesda on Waterloo Road and I spent a lot of time with them there. This became our family's place of worship although I had been christened at Cranmer Methodist Church on nearby Newhampton Road. I remember I used to play on the church organ, pulling out the stops. I have recently found out that my mother was actually a very accomplished church organist in Brewood where she grew up.

I used to go to the matinee performance at the Odeon cinema on Saturdays and later the ABC. I remember you had to go back next week to see how the cliff-hanger concluded. I also went to a stamp shop in the town centre to buy a packet of stamps every Saturday with my father. I still have the stamps. At that time Wolverhampton was charming with its shopping arcades and old buildings. I also liked going to the old open market by St Peter's church. The aerial money system in Bedford Williams was fascinating. I also enjoyed going to the Co-op and Beatties to see Father Christmas. Another Christmas tradition was to go to see the crib in St Peter's gardens with my father every Christmas while my mother cooked. In those days children seemed to find enjoyment in much simpler things. At Christmas I used to go to the Grand Theatre to see the pantomime. I usually went with a group from wherever my father was working at, at that time. Either Boulton Paul or H M Hobson, both aircraft engineering firms. After the pantomime season my mother would take me to see Peter Pan also at the Grand.

I remember the various deliveries to the house. There was the bread delivery van, Mr Lane the greengrocer with his goods on the back of his horse and cart, the milk man, the Lanes grocery delivery and the laundry man from Wolverhampton Steam Laundry. There was also Mr Purcell, from Dunstall Rd, who was a character as well as being the chimney sweep, the window cleaner, coalman and dustbin men. Everybody seemed to come to you, so every day was different.

Barbara Handley

The School closed in 1967 when everyone moved to the new West Park School in Devon Road, with the exception of the reception and nursery classes which stayed at Red Cross Street until their new buildings were opened in 1980 at Lansdowne Road. There was some use of the old school buildings by St Peter and St Paul's Church, Wulfrun College and Wolverhampton Polytechnic, before all was demolished in 1989.

19.

End of an Era

FOR ABOUT seven years life had continued straightforwardly at Red Lion Street. At some point I had been moved from the larger back bedroom to the smaller front one. The back room became used for storage, and Dad's old bicycle which he never rode again was kept in there, to gradually gather rust, along with toys and games and books of mine which would disappear if they were not played with.

We did not have much money, and it was rare for us to have anything new for the house, such as carpets, curtains, or furniture. But Mum always kept it clean and tidy, which would include the messy job of occasionally black-leading the old-fashioned grate in the dining room. She went without to ensure I had clothes to fit as I grew, and food to eat, and I would never be short of books, toys and games.

At Christmas I was pleased and satisfied with what awaited me when I went into Mum and Dad's room to see what Father Christmas had brought during the night – he was obviously grateful for the mince pie and sherry Dad had left for him the previous evening. There would be a large present, such as a toy theatre made of stiff cardboard with scenery and figures to play out a pantomime, an 00 Gauge electric train set, a Meccano set, a Bayko set. It might be a compendium of games, or a child's conjuring set. If there were any doubts about Father Christmas, one year it was proved he existed when I saw in advance the large present. It was a box containing the pieces, made of plastic, to make my own model fort or castle. It was quite a large box, and was being kept at Pinfold Lane, for Nan and Frank to send off to Father Christmas, so I was only allowed a quick peep at it. I never saw it again until it arrived on Christmas morning, so Father Christmas must have brought it. There was usually a Rupert or TV Annual or something of the kind.

On Christmas Day, weather permitting, Nan and Frank would walk the three miles from Penn to our house after lunch, as there were no buses, and stay for tea and into the early evening, when they would have to walk back. On Boxing Day, when buses did run, we would go to theirs.

The stay at Pinfold Lane was something I looked forward to each summer holiday from school. Apparently I became so excited I would even tell the Teacher that I was going to my Nan's during the holiday. I think back now that it must have been a little sad for my Mum, my having a holiday from school and immediately leaving her and home for three weeks, even if it was only three miles away, and at her mother's. But of course I was returning to my place of birth.

Here I would enjoy lots of time with Frank, when he was not at work. He was quite a regular smoker, and his empty green Woodbine packets were collected for us to make tanks. The outside of the old-style packet was cut into three pieces, fitting inside each other to form the hexagonal top part. The inside was curved to slide into this top piece at front and back to make the tread, with the thin sidepieces folded lengthways to make the guns that would poke out from the top part. We eventually had dozens of these tanks all lined up for action.

Another offshoot from his smoking was the collecting of matchboxes, to be used for building, and there must have been hundreds of these stored in a large cardboard box. They could be used as building bricks to make a house or something larger, such as a cinema or theatre – again the theatre interest. If the boxes were slotted into each other these could form beams for stretching over openings. I soon learned that you had to be careful how you put these boxes together, otherwise your walls would fall over.

In my early years, when wanting to use toy cars in a game, we invented what was called "Auntie Mary's", with playing cards laid out to make a crossroads, which is strange when you consider the centre of Tewkesbury where they lived is where three streets meet at the Cross.

One early memory at Pinfold Lane was listening to the Archers on the radio in the early evening. They had their first television after us, and before that relied on the radio. They followed the serial carefully, and so no one was allowed to speak whilst it was being broadcast. I was told that as a baby I was jogged up and down on Nan's or Frank's lap to the rhythm of the theme music.

Back in Red Lion Street, Mum and Dad's room was next to the party wall with house No 1, and the bedroom next door was the one occupied by another Tony, son of our neighbours Mr & Mrs Nicholls. Tony played electric guitar in a pop group, and would practise in his room, so of course Mum could not get to sleep until he stopped – not that it was all that late. I had a four stringed plastic guitar bought for me as a present, and Tony Nicholls attempted to teach me how to begin to play but without success. He was keen on the music of the Shadows, and his practice sessions would sometimes include a great imitation of Hank Marvin's lead guitar themes, which Mum would enjoy anyway!

We often kept a goldfish in a tank or bowl, maybe one we had won at a side stall in the fairground. If a fair was set up in or near the town centre, I would generally be taken to sample the rides and the sideshows. Usually it would be a Pat Collins' Fair, as they were the local show-people.

As for other pets, before Skippy who had the sad end, we had a large, severe, long-haired black cat, with the simple name of Tibby. Dad said this was a simplification of his full name "Tibosina Perrydarkus". He was quite an independent individual, not given to having a fuss made of him, and one day he upped sticks, wandered off and did not come back. It was decided we should have a dog as a replacement, and Skippy was just getting his feet under the table, when, unannounced, Tibby turned up on the doorstep. He was welcomed, but finding another animal had taken his place he left again, never to return.

After Skippy we had another black puppy, a crossbred Labrador Retriever, so young when he came to us, because of the sad demise of the mother of the litter, that his eyes were still closed. It was uncertain if he would survive, and Mum continued to feed him milk with a baby feeder. He was called Sooty, and he was a great pet as regards friendliness, if a little weak when it came to obedience. We took him to dog training classes at a Church Hall in Stafford Street for a while. Most of the other dogs in the class were quite reasonable in their understanding and took heed of instructions, but there was one middle-aged lady whose little dog was evidently upset by the whole thing, continually snapping and yapping. Her efforts to control it consisted of pulling on the lead and calling out "Enough! Enough!" The dog either did not understand or did not agree, as the sharp words made no difference. Sooty decided he did not wish to play any part in this education. Our participation ceased when the instructor, in the certain knowledge he knew how to get

Sooty to walk to heel, did not bargain for our smiling faithful dog's strength in pulling in the opposite direction, and he broke the lead. After this we promised Sooty he would not have to endure this again.

Sooty was to stay a part of the family for several years after we moved from Red Lion Street. He was always nervous of thunderstorms, and one day happened to be in the garden when a storm began with little warning. Despite the hedges and fences being secured he found a way through and bolted, probably at a clap of thunder or flash of lightning. Hours of searching in the rain, asking anyone we saw if they had noticed him, advertising in the newspaper, leaving details with police, were all to no avail. We just hoped that he found a good home somewhere else.

The first four houses in Red Lion Street were earmarked for demolition, not long after I began at the Grammar School in 1962. The land was proposed for redevelopment with an extension to the adjoining Telephone Exchange.

We asked to be re-housed by the Council at Warstones Estate, to be nearer to Nan and Frank in Pinfold Lane. We were offered the tenancy of a house in Rindleford Avenue, and moved there a few weeks after the beginning of the school term. The move in itself proved financially difficult, to add to the school costs already incurred. For many years now anyone displaced from their house by the Council has received the equivalent of Home Loss and Disturbance Payments. In 1962 you had to accept the first offer of accommodation, be out by a certain date, and you received no financial help whatsoever.

Because of the move to another school and house, old friendships, which had seemed destined to last forever, dwindled and died. Despite good neighbours on both sides of us, Rindleford Avenue proved a lonely place with no new friendships, and the new school also proved a difficult place in which to make friends initially.

No one ever said growing up was going to be easy. Ask any child who has been reluctant to go to school because of the need to avoid another who delights in bullying, where it seems impossible to fight back because the other is stronger, where it is not the "done thing" to tell tales; even where the bullying amounts to continued assaults which leave their scars, physically and mentally, for years. In my case, I did have an older boy who intervened, on seeing the assault once, and threatened the perpetrator if he should see him do it again.

Already the Town Centre was changing, with the construction of the first and then the second part of the Ring Road, the grand Victorian Market Hall had been demolished, and the new one had opened, and other modern buildings were springing up. The 1960s were in the opinion of many a disaster for altering the character of the town and the loss of so many old friends in buildings. But if you speak to anyone who lived in a town or city at the time they will say the same about the effects of the 1960s on their own urban areas.

Red Lion Street has changed so much since those days. There are no houses, the Telephone Exchange dominates, no alley leads up to the Catholic Church, and the end of the street was chopped off by the Ring Road. The Catholic Church and Presbytery were restored, and the cemetery remains, however. After the restoration it was much cleaned up, with benches and planting, and the gravestones were neatly arranged. Whilst it is now closed off and inaccessible, it was for some years open for all to use as a quiet haven, with no one threatening that you would "catch the fever in there!" On my visits there at that time, as I stood in the clean and tidy space and looked around it, I wondered how many ghosts of the 1950s children still chased around at play, in blissful ignorance of the future.

Tony helping step-grandfather on his allotment behind Pinfold Lane.